"Mendelsohn's sophisticated inquiry into homosexuality, identity, and language is so lovingly integrated into this memoir that intellectual explorations seem to be as much a part of his life as his family and his lovers are. . . . His etymological investigations and his readings of Catullus and Sappho are curiously tender, and make the memories—of a college love for a beautiful swim-team boy, for instance, or of a trickster grandfather—even more affecting."   —*The New Yorker*

"In this symphonic meditation on identity, an autobiography only for lack of a richer word, Mendelsohn uses the grammatical peculiarity of the 'middle voice' in Greek, which he describes as a sort of shimmering synthesis of not quite compatible conditions, as a metaphor for the levels of self within him. . . . Mendelsohn reads himself and the widening spiral around him—of family, friends, lovers, society, culture—as a vast and complex text. Aggressively honest, deeply perceptive, and quite beautiful."   —*The Boston Globe*

"A brilliant tale of personal discovery."   —*Interview*

"It is difficult to believe that this is Mr. Mendelsohn's first book: there is a lifetime of thinking in it that hints at his having written a great many more. Mr. Mendelsohn does not have an ounce of self-pity on his learned bones, which means that it is a pleasure to read about his experiences because they are what book reviewers used to call 'universal' without quite knowing what that meant. Daniel Mendelsohn does: he is a citizen of the world. This book is equal to Whitman's 'Song of Myself,' and it is just as edifying and moving and true."   —Hilton Als

"A startling, intimate and original work. . . . A remarkable tapestry, weaving family and personal memoir, ancient mythology, and a meditation on the meaning of self. . . . Unapologetic, honest and revealing . . . Mendelsohn's language is exquisite, and deserves to be savored, word by word, page by page."   —*Minneapolis Star Tribune*

"*The Elusive Embrace* introduces a unique and irresistible voice—erudite, explicit, tender, and wise. Daniel Mendelsohn's personal odyssey of the double life, with his discovery of fatherhood and its illumination of a profound male identity that transcends traditional categories . . . heralds a new century of sexual understanding. An instant classic."
                          —Elaine Showalter

"[This] book offers as intelligible, morally and spiritually honest an explication of what it is like to be a male homosexual in American society today as we are going to find."
                          —*The Washington Times*

"*The Elusive Embrace* is an eerily beautiful book. Daniel Mendelsohn's intelligence, lovely sensibility, and style each deserve the laurel wreath."   —Louis Begley

DANIEL MENDELSOHN

THE ELUSIVE EMBRACE

Daniel Mendelsohn was born on Long Island in 1960 and studied Classics at the University of Virginia and at Princeton. His reviews and essays on literary and cultural subjects appear regularly in numerous publications, including *The New Yorker*, *The New York Review of Books*, and *The New York Times*. His books include the international bestseller *The Lost: A Search for Six of Six Million*, which won the National Book Critics Circle Award, the Prix Médicis, and many other honors; a collection of essays, *How Beautiful It Is and How Easily It Can Be Broken*; and, most recently, his acclaimed translations of C. P. Cavafy's *Collected Poems* and *The Unfinished Poems*. Mr. Mendelsohn is also the recipient of a Guggenheim Fellowship, the National Book Critics Circle Citation for Excellence in Book Reviewing, and the George Jean Nathan Award for Dramatic Criticism. He teaches at Bard College.

THE ELUSIVE EMBRACE

Desire and the Riddle of Identity

DANIEL MENDELSOHN

VINTAGE BOOKS

A Division of Random House, Inc.

New York

FIRST VINTAGE BOOKS EDITION, JUNE 2000

Copyright © 1999 by Daniel Mendelsohn

All rights reserved under International and Pan-American Copyright Conventions. Published in the United States by Vintage Books, a division of Random House, Inc., New York, and simultaneously in Canada by Random House of Canada Limited, Toronto. Originally published in hardcover in the United States by Alfred A. Knopf, a division of Random House, Inc., New York, in 1999.

A portion of "Paternities" was previously published in slightly different form as "Notes from an Unlikely Father" in *Out* magazine.

Some of the names and biographical details in this memoir have been changed.

The Library of Congress has cataloged the Knopf edition as follows:
Mendelsohn, Daniel Adam, 1960–
The elusive embrace: desire and the riddle of identity / Daniel Mendelsohn
p. cm.
ISBN: 0-375-40095-8
1. Mendelsohn, Daniel Adam. 2. Gay men—United States—Biography.
3. Jewish gays —United States —Biography. 4. Gays—Identity. 5. Jews—Identity.
I. Title.
HQ75.8.M46 A3 1999
99-62633
CIP

Vintage ISBN: 978-0-375-70697-4

Author photograph © Marion Ettlinger
Book design by Dorothy S. Baker

www.vintagebooks.com

20 19 18 17 16 15 14 13 12 11

148315157

Only he who knows what longing is,
knows what I suffer.

Goethe, *Die Sehnsucht*

What is the riddle behind it?

Socrates, in Plato's *Apology*

CONTENTS

THE ELUSIVE EMBRACE

1. GEOGRAPHIES

For a long time I have lived in two places.

One of these places is a quiet street lined with houses whose windows peer out from between wooden shutters at trees and the occasional car, a street in many ways like the nondescript one where I grew up, seething and afraid. When I am in that place, I live in one of those narrow squinting houses with a woman and a small child. I will come to that later.

The other place where I live is in New York City, slightly to the north of gay culture.

Half a block west of my front door lies Eighth Avenue, a one-way, four-lane, north-south artery that carries traffic uptown—that is, north. Eighth Avenue begins far downtown as the much smaller Hudson Street, still paved in places with cobblestones and endlessly subject to obscure and ongoing repairs; down there, it takes you past tiny cross-streets whose numberless names betray their great age, since once you get above the Village, above Fourteenth Street, the later, modern, rigid grid on which Manhattan is laid out supersedes the haphazard and twisted and ancient streets to the south. The grid is, for the most part, easy: its longitudinal lines are all called avenues, their numbers increasing as you go from east to west (with a few famous exceptions, like Park and Madison), and its latitudinal lines are streets, whose numbers escalate as you go from south to north. Attempts are occasionally made to impose names on these numbers—we are supposed to call Sixth Avenue "the Avenue of the Americas," for instance, and someone has rechristened a snippet of West Sixty-fifth Street near Lincoln Center "Leonard Bernstein Way"—but New Yorkers, always pressed for time, enjoy the brisk and unromantic efficiency of the numbers and ignore the names. In many ways we are a city of people who prefer numbers to names.

As Hudson Street arcs its way up through the West Village, which until recently was the center of New York gay life, it shakes off its curves and widens, becoming Eighth Avenue just below Fourteenth Street, which is the east-west thoroughfare that marks the southern boundary of the neighborhood called Chelsea, the current center of New York gay life. Fourteenth Street divides the Village from Chelsea. Most of the streets in Greenwich Village have names; all of the streets in Chelsea are numbered.

If you walk the half-block from my door to Eighth Avenue and make a right turn into it here, in the mid-Twenties, following the traffic north, it'll take you first past some nondescript lofts and tenements and, at Twenty-seventh Street, the Fashion Institute of Technology, which is known generally by its acronym, F.I.T., or, more locally, as "Fags In Training"; then it heads past the big train station at Thirty-fourth Street and the bus station at Forty-second. The avenue continues up through the glittering clutter of Times Square and, after dissolving briefly into the incoherent rapids of Columbus Circle, reemerges rather grandly as Central Park West. Lined by stout matronly prewar buildings on one side and the park on the other, Central Park West neatly divides Culture from Nature for the perusal of those well heeled enough to appreciate the view. It continues with bourgeois rectitude straight up along the park into the West Seventies and Eighties and Nineties— addresses that, at least until the rise of Chelsea as the city's premier gay neighborhood, were favored by a lot of gay men, but are now more likely to be associated, at least by the émigrés here in my neighborhood, with yuppies, strollers, and, vaguely, heterosexuality.

But of course I rarely turn right at the end of my block. Instead I almost always head south, against the flow of traffic. When I do so it's only a couple of blocks from my street to Twenty-third Street, which is Chelsea's northern border. The neighborhood itself extends as far east as Broadway and as far west as Tenth Avenue; but its living heart is Eighth Avenue. Between Fourteenth Street on the south and Twenty-third Street on the north, Eighth Avenue is, for all intents and purposes, the Main Street of the gayest enclave of the gayest city in the world.

When I was in high school, in a newish suburb that had the word "Old" in its name, as if to assuage the insecurities of its first-generation American homeowners, a place where the houses, identical in structure, were distinguishable only by the color of their nonfunctional shutters, I dreamed of a place like this. I am sure that many other gay youths had (and still have) the same dream. Like me, they may have secretly read certain books over the course of successive weekends while standing nervously in the stacks of the local public library or in B. Dalton, so great was the terror of bringing those particular books home; like me, they may have kissed and fondled the soft demanding bodies of girls with the same sense of willed detachment they brought to laboratory dissections of frogs; like me, they may have needed to summon up the pictures of other classmates as they did so, classmates who were also boys, whose striped swimsuits and wide, awkward shoulders gave some of their friends a sense of panicked tenderness that, because unutterable, soon hardened into irony. I secretly imagined a place where all the people were other boys, and where all the stores and books and songs and movies and restaurants were by boys, about other boys. It would be a place where somehow the outside reality of the world that met your eyes and ears could finally be made to match the inner, hidden reality of what you knew yourself to be. A place where willed detachment and a carapace of irony would no longer be necessary.

This is the place I can go to if, when I reach the end of my street, I turn left instead of right. Curiously, now that I'm here it's not clear to me that this is the place I want to be. I divide my time now between my two geographies: the familiar streets of Chelsea, with its men and boys and flesh, and the street in the suburb about sixty miles away, lined with pin oaks and taciturn old houses. In front of these houses you will see no young men. You might see a retired widower mowing the lawn—"cutting the grass," he might say—with a rusting red mower, or an old woman sitting on the porch, fanning herself with a tabloid, scanning the street and other people's windows for some event, something to happen. Built long before the thinly shingled houses in the place where I grew up were hastily assembled, these houses are stolid: you sense about them that they know they will outlive, once again, the present generation of owners. These houses have real shutters, shutters that work.

Sometimes when I take a break from writing I walk down the east side of Eighth to Fourteenth Street, then cross over to the west side and walk back up. At the corner of Twenty-second Street is the Big Cup, a Day-Glo–painted coffeehouse that has proved even more popular as a late-night alternative to gay bars than it is as an afternoon gathering spot for other self-employeds. The latter tend, as far as I can see, to fall into two groups: writers, whose elaborate charade of using their laptops productively sags more and more with every hopeful glance up at the opening door, and a small but fairly regular collection of hustlers, who monopolize the telephone at the back of the room while checking off entries in what you assume must be small black books. In Twenty-second Street itself are Barracuda, a low-ceilinged gay bar that has been frequented exclusively by horny young middle-class gay men since it opened in the fall of 1995 with a party celebrating the publication of a queer-radical treatise by the lesbian activist Urvashi Vaid; and Barracuda's next-door neighbor, a bookstore called the Unicorn, whose inconsequential stock lines a small front room through which you pass en route to the back room, a barely lit space where men can have sex with each other after paying a ten-dollar entrance fee.

But as I say, I usually continue straight down Eighth. Just past the Big Cup is a home furnishings store called Distinctive Furnishings, where you can buy, among other things, screen savers that display mostly-naked, muscle-bound young men in bathing suits. Then there's a clothing store called Tops N Bottoms (a gleeful double entendre: in the language of gay sex those words refer to those who prefer the active and passive roles in intercourse). A nearby card store called Rainbows and Triangles has a full stock of gay-themed birthday and anniversary and condolence cards. "Because I know how you feel" goes the inside of a card whose outside shows a well-dressed young hunk in a black suit holding a white rose. On this side of the avenue you eventually also pass the American Fitness gym, almost invariably referred to by its campier nickname, "American Princess." Many of the gyms frequented by gay men have been similarly redubbed: Better Bodies has become "Bitter Bottoms," and, in wry but not wholly unadmiring tribute to its owner's hypertrophied pectorals, the David Barton gym on the corner of Sixth Avenue and Thirteenth Street is also known as "Dolly Parton's." A bit farther south is the Chelsea Gym, through whose enormous second-floor windows you can watch men cycle and lift things and run. The crucial meeting between the two male leads in the gay film *Jeffrey* is set here. Perhaps in recognition of its primacy in the chronology of body culture, the Chelsea Gym has no nickname.

Also on this side of Eighth Avenue are the Viceroy restaurant—a place you hear described as being one of the "nice" eating spots on this avenue which seems, the more you think of it, to be about little besides feeding, developing, and clothing men's bodies—and the Video Blitz video store. The Video Blitz is just across Seventeenth Street from a huge Blockbuster, but local gay men are apt to belong to both, since Blockbuster cannot compete with Video Blitz's ample collection of art films and gay pornography for rental: *The Bigger the Better, A Matter of Size, Brothers Should Do It*.

When I get as far south as Fourteenth Street I usually cross Eighth Avenue and head back uptown. At Fifteenth I pass the

Candy Bar and Grill, which opened in the fall of 1996 and whose door is monitored alternately by a tallish drag queen and a shorter, chubby club promoter. The décor here recalls that of upscale Catskills hotels of the fifties, the kind of place my Jewish, heterosexual family might have gone for a weekend in, say, 1953, the year my parents, a mathematician and a schoolteacher, were married; but by now the large and intricate "Moderne" lighting fixtures that would have impressed those young Jewish people almost fifty years ago have, like so many artifacts from the world of their youth, somehow become the objects of irony, signaling a particular brand of stylishness, a certain kind of knowingness, to the young, attractive gay men who come here in order to feel glamorous and special. (For some reason many of these men are dark-haired; not Jewish perhaps, but Mediterranean.) North of Candy Bar is FoodBar, perhaps the most popular restaurant in the neighborhood, at least partly because its co-owner, Joe, is as opulently well muscled and darkly handsome as some of its clientele is, and most of its clientele aspires to be. As you walk past FoodBar you invariably see him through the enormous plate-glass window etched with the restaurant's name; he's sitting on a bar stool close to the front door, smoking in a tight T-shirt, dispensing seats and air kisses to huge men in work boots and tank tops. Often as I pass by on my walks he'll raise an amused eyebrow at me and beckon me in with a look that says he won't take seriously my inevitable protests about overwork and looming deadlines; pushing a pack of cigarettes across the bar at me, he'll order me a glass of red wine, and another one for himself, and we'll gossip about boys or books. There are no unattractive waiters at FoodBar.

Just past FoodBar, heading north again on Eighth, is Eighteenth and Eighth, a neighborhood standby with a slightly

different, less intricately muscled clientele than the one at
FoodBar; you sense that the staff here is more familiar with
show tunes than with extended-play dance remixes of *I Am
What I Am*. After this, it's a pretty barren stretch back up to
Twenty-third—although, perversely, this seems to be the
cruisiest stretch of street in the neighborhood, perhaps because
pedestrians are more likely to be looking straight ahead than
into storefronts.

The corner of Twenty-third and Eighth is the one my friends
and I only half-jokingly refer to as Intersection of Desire. Here
I've occasionally met, and subsequently gone home with, total
strangers whom I've found attractive. At the southwest corner
of this intersection stands a building that some people I know
call Trick Towers, a building where I have in fact had sex with
strangers, a building, too, where a handsome man I'd met and
found myself liking once, a successful young executive who
secretly wrote sad poems while he was away on business trips,
lived and continued to live after ceasing, abruptly, to return my
calls. (This is the other, flip side of tricking.) The first stranger
I met in this way, on this corner, after I'd moved to Chelsea,
ignorant of what it had become since the last time I'd lived in
New York—I was merely relieved, after that long time out of
town, to have found an apartment so easily, the apartment of a
friend of a friend, the latter a woman who introduced me to a
roommate whom I slept with for a while and who has since
died; the former, a woman whose brother died, too—the first
stranger I'd met in this way was a dark-eyed, dark-haired
Cuban whom I passed one day on my way home from Food-
Bar. He didn't seem Latin to me. Something about his compact

frame and the set of his broken-looking nose made me think that he could have been one of my Jewish relatives.

It was a classic cruise, with its own predictable choreography. After exchanging looks, we went on walking a few steps; then each turned round to make sure that the other was watching; then we both walked a few more steps; and finally turned round and walked back toward each other, with protectively ironic grins. He was en route to an appointment, he told me, but would I like to meet at that same corner later that evening, at six? I would. We met at six, and went back to his place, which turned out to be a half-block from mine; but not before we'd walked around the block once or twice. This was before I got used to the swift efficiency of street cruising, before I realized that "preliminaries" were a holdover from that other world I'd inhabited, the one with girls in it, where sex was the conclusion rather than the premise of erotic interaction. We talked for perhaps four minutes before he put his hand on my thigh; about his family in Queens, from whom he'd fled as soon as he was old enough to get a job. After we'd finished, I asked for a glass of water, and while we very briefly stood in the kitchen, noticeably less comfortable with each other fully clothed than we'd been while naked in his bed, I admired the sleek rubber mats that hid the ancient Formica on his kitchen counters. As I left he was recommending places where I could get them myself, cheap.

My taste in men runs to extreme likeness or extreme difference. The Latino with the inky eyes, whose name I can't remember if indeed I ever knew it, was compact and dark, and so could not have been more different from another boy I picked up at the intersection of Twenty-third and Eighth about a year later. This other boy was a tall, smoothly muscled blond called Mike, whose backwards baseball cap struck me, for once, as appealingly authentic. I won't pretend that this didn't add to his allure for me—this, despite the fact that, all too predictably, he was an aspiring actor and model. That much was easy enough to believe. His features were solemn and regular, and he swung unself-consciously into the loose-hipped *contrapposto* favored by the models who appear in Obsession ads. There is a pose in Greek sculpture of the high classical period called *diadoumenos*: an athlete stands with arms raised, tying a ribbon around his head. At one point in our conversation Mike reached up with both hands to straighten his cap; if you squinted, the comparison wasn't too much of a stretch.

At the time I met this boy I was working on an article about the movement of openly gay men out of gay ghettos like this one and back to the suburban neighborhoods where they'd grown up. During the writing of this piece I'd gone for a walk; after chatting with Joe at FoodBar, I was returning to my place when Mike and I passed each other. The little pas de deux followed. But between the Cuban and Mike there had been a number—neither tiny nor vast—of chance meetings at or near the corner of Twenty-third Street and Eighth. This time, it was he who insisted on walking around the block several times before returning to my place—an exercise that seemed to me at the time to have less to do with any effort on his part to ascertain that I wasn't somehow dangerous, as had been the case when I'd met the Cuban the summer before, than with some other, hidden, interior attempt to exorcise something else, something darker and less easy to articulate.

During this walk Mike, who at twenty-five was ten years younger than I, asked me what I did, and when I told him what I was writing about—in the vaguest possible way, since

I didn't want to get side-tracked from the real, tacit subject of our conversation—he became, for the first time, really engaged. He spoke, now, animatedly, telling me in a rush that he himself was moving back to the St. Louis suburb he'd grown up in, and that this was his last day in New York. He said that he'd felt overwhelmed by the dizzying nightlife, by the sheer, confusing superabundance of opportunities. "I need to get my head together," he told me, reaching up again to adjust his baseball cap, as if it could reconnect him with some reassuring reality from his childhood: playing catch with his father, maybe, or Little League. We walked and talked a little more and finally went back to my place. As he climaxed he had an oddly abstracted look, as though he were trying to remember something very important. He dressed quickly while we both tried to make conversation to ease the space between my bed and the door. He talked some more about why he was leaving New York City. "I came here to find myself," he said as he walked from the front door of my apartment to the elevator across the hall, "but instead, I got lost."

In the surviving sculptures of the *diadoumenos* type, such as a Roman copy of one done by the acclaimed Athenian sculptor Polyclitus, which I have stared at in the National Archeological Museum in Athens, willing the stone to mean something more than itself, the forearms and hands have snapped off above the crooked elbows, leaving the figure with upraised stumps that rise parallel to the upper torso. By no means an infrequent accident of time—extremities are always the first things to break off, or to erode—this alteration has, in the case of these particular sculptures, transformed what was supposed to be a stance conveying casual assurance into one of helpless astonishment, or despair.

The walk with Mike reminded me of something; it wasn't

until much later that I realized what it was. Thirty years earlier, on a cold brilliant day in February, my mother and grandfather had walked three times around the block, past the houses with their different-colored shutters. They had just finished sitting shivah for my grandmother. She, as it happens, had walked with me often around the same block while I, a skinny child of four, clung to her plump diabetic forearm. My grandmother would walk me to the local park and there she'd watch me rock back and forth, a slight mouse-haired boy on a heavy painted metal horse that was mounted on a single stout spring. When we returned from the park I would sit with her on a webbed lawn chair on the broad concrete front step of my parents' house, playing with her earrings, chunky masses of beads and crystal that now lie, unused since then, in my mother's jewel box. Her earlobes were as soft as fruit. More often, it was my grandfather who would sit here, solid and proprietary in his immaculate clothes, his razor-creased trousers and his snap-brim hat, surveying the lawns and sprinklers, congratulating himself, perhaps, on the good fortune of his only child, his daughter, the vivacious kindergarten teacher with the unpredictable sense of humor who'd worn men's suits, made for her by an uncle who was a master tailor, to high school; who in her college yearbook claimed "Spelunking" as a hobby and "Taxidermy" as a career goal; who did the uncanny Dietrich imitations, singing in her deep contralto certain risqué songs in German which she would later sing to her five children in lieu of lullabies; who knew Bette Davis movies by heart; and who had, finally, married a man who could give her a house trimmed with green and fed by hissing hoses, a house with trees and with grass . . . When my mother's father was not there, on the front step, surveying, thinking perhaps of his own lost green landscapes ("It was a wonderful place for picknicks," he'd once written to me of the village in the Carpathian Mountains he'd left in 1920), my grandmother and I would sneak into his chair and sit quietly as I stroked her ears and she did what she had always done, which was to wait for him to return and claim his place.

Now, a year later, it was she who was finally the object of attention, the cause for all the movement. Now my mother was telling me that she and my grandfather were taking her dead mother's soul to heaven. The distance it took them to do so is slightly longer than the last leg of my habitual circuit down and then back up Eighth Avenue—the distance that gets you from the Intersection of Desire back to my place.

The first time I ever had the experience of desiring another man who I knew also desired me was when I was in college, and I walked aimlessly for many hours one day a long time ago, following him. We were both nineteen, and I never knew his name. He was waiting at the farthest edge of the university cemetery, a spot where the graves become indistinguishable from the woods.

This was at a college in the South; these woods were thick, choked with creepers and dense with trees you won't find in the suburbs of Long Island. It was a strange place for someone like me to have ended up. I'd come here, to the university nested in the foothills of the Blue Ridge, because in high school I'd loved a boy who'd come from this state, a boy who shunned me when he realized I wanted him; I thought that by going here, to the place where he was from, I could recuperate him somehow, have a part of him. I thought that being in this place, with its hills and horse farms and the smoky blue spine that was the mountain range in the distance, would let me experience him, finally. My choice of universities had struck people I grew up with as strange; no one else in my graduating high school class of five hundred had even applied here; the South, it was felt, was hostile to Jews. On Long Island, the South required some explanation. Of course I would not tell them that I was going there because of a boy with shiny yellow hair, and so I would observe that the university I'd chosen had a renowned English department. It was always assumed that I would be an English major, and this seemed to satisfy people.

But whatever I told them, and myself, I soon felt at home here, against all expectations. Here I would go to the parties attended by fair-haired boys so attenuated that their khakis and pink Oxford-cloth button-down shirts would flap about their bodies like flags as they talked about the places they came from, places familiar to each other but strange and beautiful-sounding to me, who grew up in a place that had not existed until the month before I was born. They talked about towns where their families had lived for ten generations. I visited their houses, houses that had family cemeteries on the grounds, saw over the mantels the portraits of handsome dead soldiers wearing the uniforms of a defeated nation, understood that for the women (whom I did not desire but whose carefully tended beauty still had some effect on me) the elaborate standards for beauty and social comportment that they applied only slightly more harshly to others than to themselves were not detachable from the rest of their lives, but were, like their houses and the family names they kept passing on, the means by which they asserted who they were, what culture and history they belonged to. Here was a culture I could understand, one that had created a great romance out of a great defeat, a civilization that had been able to endure loss and real privation

because it believed in its own myth of lost beauty, the possession of which, however brief and however long ago, elevated
the lovely and effete vanquished far above the crass, practical
victors. This was a fable I had heard before, at my grandfather's
knee, as he told me about his family, a family of delicate beau-
ties victimized by war, by unexpected poverty, by the cynical
maneuverings of more practical, less genteel relatives; and it
was one I would unconsciously seek out again, here at college,
in studying the Greeks, another defeated nation that clung,
through misery, to the belief that she was superior to her
victor. *Graecia capta ferum victorem cepit et artes / intulit agresti
Latio . . . ,* the Roman poet Horace wrote: "Captive Greece
conquered her savage captor, and brought the arts into wild
Italy." Southern culture, I found, made sense to me.

So here I stood in this cemetery by the thick wood, staring
at this boy. I had seen him before. Around campus, in classrooms, at parties, he would appear like an optical trick, or a
symptom of some strange new disease of the eye, seeming to
exist only at the periphery of my own field of vision, edging
his way out of a lecture hall just as I entered, or unfolding himself from a narrow plastic library chair precisely at the moment
I'd pass by, making my way silently through the stacks as if the
thing I was looking for was a book. It was in the library that I'd
see him most often, and whenever I did pass him there, only to
see him leave moments later, I'd be careful to express ostentatious disappointment at not having found the volume I was
supposed to have been looking for—just enough to convince
anyone who might be watching that it was, after all, merely a
book I wanted. I'd gesture impatiently at an imaginary space
on a stack, or shake my head as if confounded by the incompe-
tence of the staff. At the time all this took place, when I was

nineteen and twenty and then twenty-one, I may have convinced myself that all this show was meant to fool other people—people who might have some sly, secret knowledge all their own (upperclassmen? faculty?) and who were sure to have guessed at the motives for my furtive movements through these many miles of books. But now I am not so sure.

What I did realize, even then, was that after a few months of these seemingly chance meetings, I'd developed an ambulatory tic. Each time I entered or left a class or dining hall, I'd suddenly slow my steps, as you would slow down a film, in order better to pinpoint the precise moment when this tall and unknown boy—whose friends were not my friends, whose dark hair always falling over one eye left me feeling choked, both elated and needy—would suddenly appear.

I knew he knew I was watching him. During the spring of my second year, there was an early evening when I was at a party in a garden charged with the surprisingly green and oniony smell of magnolia blossoms that have been crushed underfoot. Under the trees you could see duos and trios of undergraduates, their voices uneven with drink and the anticipation of sex. From where I sat, on a bench nearly hidden among some low shrubs near an undulating serpentine wall—*only one brick thick*, the students who were University Guides would knowingly point out—I could focus, without being seen, on one group of three. They were two boys and a girl whose back was to me. She had on an off-white dress; blond tendrils floated from her damp pink neck. Beneath one of her creamy shoes there protruded the pointed edge of a black silk bowtie, like an unhealthy tongue under a pale upper lip. One of the boys was kneeling in mock supplication, yanking at the black tongue: whatever the game was, it was clear that she'd won. As he bent to retrieve the tie he suddenly looked up, straight at me. Obviously it was he. His eyes were no particular color—dark without being actually brown, the color of seaweed when it's still wet with the ocean. These eyes and my own locked so emphatically you could almost hear the *click*.

All of this took a few seconds, but it was enough; in the moment we looked at each other, there was a perfect complicity between us, clear as speech. Afterwards he suddenly rose and, turning away from me, handed the tie back to his friend. But the gesture was slack; the fun had gone out of their play. I alone was satisfied, because I understood then that another game had just begun, and that he and I were the only ones playing.

Now, six months later, he was standing at the edge of a graveyard whose neglected headstones staggered above the October mud like crooked teeth in bad gums. It was the time of year when midterm exams were given, but no one was ever quite sure whether it was this, or the fact that during this season the rain fell so unrelentingly and the sky lost its sun, that had inspired several generations of students, but mostly freshmen, to dub these wet Shenandoah autumns "suicide weather." Everywhere there was mud: on the elaborately patterned brick walkways that took you to the brick-and-plaster neoclassical buildings where classes were held, on the floors of dorm rooms and dining halls, caked on your shoes (Top-Siders, duck boots), licking your socks through the soles, plastering the cuffs of your pants. We first-yearmen thought suicide weather was a joke until halfway through that first autumn, when a sophomore in a dorm called Bonnycastle—or maybe it was the dorm next door, the one that housed the student radio station where I deejayed from six to nine in the morning—shotgunned himself after midterms. Our jokes became warier, and we worked harder.

I'd come to the graveyard on an errand that hadn't struck me, at the time, as being macabre—an assignment given by a classics professor. He was a young but already failed man who wore his razor-pleated khakis and Harris tweed coats, with their careful decorative elbow patches, as if they could some-how armor him against the indignities of the tenure process. Young as we were, those of us who sat twice a week in his second-year Greek-prose seminar reading Socrates' elegant and fruitless speech of self-defense already understood that this man was somehow a failure, and the knowledge occasionally made us cruel; not everything we muttered as we made our agonizing way through Plato's *Apology* was a translation from the Greek. This man—whom I did not like then and who has since died, still fairly young, bequeathing his library to the graduate students of the university where, as it happened, I would eventually go to do my graduate work in classics, and where, with a complex emotion that my fellow students could not share, I hauled away my allotted share of books from this bequest (Drees's *Olympia,* Fränkel on Horace), no less greedy for my secret guilt—this man had challenged us to locate a tomb. It was the grave of an eminent nineteenth-century clas-sicist whose epitaph, we'd been told, was a line from a tragedy. We were to find the grave and copy the epitaph; then translate it. I can't now recall whether there was a reward for doing so.

I didn't see my classmates creeping around on this par-ticular Saturday afternoon as I was doing, struggling with medicinal-smelling ivy that sucked at the headstones and left tiny brownish hickeys on the rock when you finally pulled it away. But then, the professor's request had probably struck me as less odd than it might have seemed to the three other stu-dents in our intermediate Greek class. By that time I'd grown used to graves. A few years earlier I'd spent a summer scraping ivy from the headstones of my relatives in some very different cemeteries, in the vast and overcrowded Jewish graveyards that form an immense, almost pharaonic necropolis that straddles the border between Brooklyn and Queens. Mount Judah, Cypress Hills: I eventually came to know the biblical and classical provenances of these names, but until then they seemed apt enough captions. Indifferent trees and dead rock were all you could see here.

Yet in the cluttered profusion of these high, narrow stones, now addressing their bilingual eulogies to the exhaust fumes of passing cars, it was as if you could glimpse a shadow of the tenemented lives these dead had lived. As, for example, there had lived my grandfather's sister, dead in 1923 at twenty-six, a week (so the story went) before her wedding. There is a monument to her here, towards the back of our large family plot. Of gray granite, it takes the form of a tree trunk whose few incipient branches are cut off abruptly at the top, a couple of heads higher than a tall man stands. At eye level, in a groin formed by two sculpted branches, an oval piece of porcelain is set; onto it a photograph of this young woman had somehow been transferred. It is the same image that had hung, much enlarged, in my grandfather's Bronx apartment, until his adolescent daughter's protests brought it down. ("Why always pictures of the *dead*?," my mother would complain.) In the three-quarter pose that best advertised her famous deep-set eyes and overripe Edwardian jawline, my great-aunt, more than a decade younger in this picture than I am now as I write, looks pensive, though not unamused—as if she'd known all along what it was she'd been posing for, and hadn't, in the end, really minded.

Already at an early age—eleven, twelve?—I was drawn to this grave, with its overdetermined iconography of beauty and loss, the intact porcelain and the truncated stone. Although it was always the last on the list of those we must visit each year—other, more recent griefs had priority—it was nonetheless the one I'd examine most eagerly. Slowly, with pleasure, my fingers would trace the crisp undulations of the Hebrew characters, which in contrast to that ironic and eloquent face would remain mute until the day when my grandfather hastily translated for me the rock's brief advertisement—that this was the grave of a virgin, *ha'betulah,* of a girl who had died before her marriage. The stone doesn't report what my grandfather, who carefully taught me his family's history and its myths, later told me, many times: that the marriage was an arranged one, the bride given to her rich cousin in exchange for ship's passages to America for the rest of her impoverished family; that the bride was tall and beautiful and the groom hunchbacked and scarred by smallpox; that after the bride's unexpected death her younger sister was later forced to marry the same man, thereby acquitting her family's debt to his family; that this sister would also die too young, tragically. These were messy lives; the inscription maintains a stony decorum.

Years after these visits to the cemetery, when I was a graduate student making guilty use of the books left by that other, less loved teacher, I would write a dissertation about, among other things, the figure of the "bride of death" in Greek tragedy—about girls who (like Sophocles' Antigone, for example) die just before marriage, sacrificing themselves for their families, their cities, sometimes their honor. I can't think, now, why I'd never made the connection before. And at the same time that I was unconsciously pursuing the figure of my dead and beautiful Jewess in pagan texts transmitted first by Alexandrian scholars and then by Greek Orthodox monks, I'd begun writing about gay culture, too, and so would spend a great deal of time looking at images of, and reading texts by and about, young people, mostly men, who had also died too soon: the beautiful dead "Greeks" of our age, Mark Doty's latter-day Alexandrians. But clearly it was much earlier, before my taste for the classics or indeed for other men had budded—the two are intertwined in my mind, the pagan culture and the pagan acts—that I first knew the allure that clings to the histories of beauty and loss. It was here, in this overcrowded ghetto of the immigrant Jewish dead, that I first knew the pleasure in deciphering narratives, in unraveling charged and secret meanings from the sinuous scripts in which they'd been furled.

So I did not find my Greek professor's challenge strange, that day in 1980. It was just after I found the inscription I was looking for, partly obscured by earth that had risen, like a loaf, around the base of the stone, that I saw the boy standing at the edge of this Virginia graveyard, and knew that he was waiting for me to follow.

I followed him that day, into the woods and past dormitories, into the absurd hat-shaped snack bar where he ordered a coffee, sat at a table watching me watch him, and then left again, with me close behind. He never turned, nor did I ever accelerate my steps. After half an hour of this he made his way into a dormitory that turned out to be located just next to the cemetery: we had traveled a great, ragged circle. This was the dormitory—one of a group called the "old dorms"—in whose basement was housed the university radio station where I worked. On the same underground level were some men's bathrooms, and occasionally some boy, wearing nothing more than a towel and the easy uninhibitedness about their bodies that straight men always seem to me to have, would wander past as I loaded an LP onto the turntable platter, and I would crane my neck, not caring about the music. It was here that my boy stopped, on this day, and for the first time turned round and looked at me, who had been tracking him. But although I'd been fearless following him outside, I was afraid to follow him inside: this, I knew with absolute certainty, was what he wanted me to do. I didn't go. I didn't go, because although I didn't know exactly what would happen if I did, I knew that to go that day would have been to commit myself to something irreversible and, worse, namable. For a long moment we stood opposite each other. I was thinking that if I could only say something, I might rescue all this for some other day when I would know what to do, be less foolish. But my voice had gone. So after giving me a look perfumed with both irony and impatience, he went inside, and I went back into the graveyard, charged and spent, and copied down the epitaph I'd been searching for. It was a line from Aeschylus: "Life is a brief encampment."

I didn't see him again after that—it was as if he'd dissolved at this moment of near contact, the way your own image reflected in still water shudders and disintegrates when you reach out to touch it. But now, twenty years and hundreds of boys later, I can see his squarish face quite clearly before me: the glossy dark-auburn hair that falls over his forehead, one stray lock hanging like an upside-down question mark; the searching sockets and their widely spaced, indeterminate eyes; the lips and cheeks that have the same high improbable color of the lips and cheeks you see in eighteenth-century French portraits, whose subjects stare out at you with the self-satisfied completeness of the dead. He himself seems now as completely present and yet as utterly remote as those people, more alive as an object for my contemplation than I allowed him to be when his flesh and blood were available to mine. This phantom is the thing that drives me to follow those other boys, into whose houses I now so easily go; and I often think that some secret image like this must lie behind the eyes of most other gay men I know, who also seem always to be restlessly seeking something, something that eludes them at the moment they possess it. Desire is movement rather than place. But even more, the memory of that long and haphazard pursuit speaks of a certain kind of relation to the rest of the world: experience rejected in favor of remembrance, the center rejected in favor of the margin. A sense of the beautiful hovering just beyond your reach, to be reflected upon and considered. The reflection becomes, in its own way, another kind of possessing.

A reflection is irresistible because it is a paradox: an opposite that is the same, an other that is also clearly your self.

The ancient Greek tendency to bipolar thinking—on the one hand *x,* but on the other hand *y;* the Greeks pushed on, but the Trojans fought back; *ouranía Aphrodité,* spiritual love, *pandêmos Aphrodité,* the common love you find on the streets, as Plato tells us—is reflected in the structure of the language itself. One of the first things you learn when you learn classical Greek, as I did during suicide weather when I was eighteen, is the existence of two untranslatable monosyllables—particles, they are called, not really full-fledged words at all—whose presence in any given sentence tells you about the balance of that sentence, what its rhythm and, ultimately, its meaning will be. Each of these two particles is always the second word in whatever clause it appears. The first of these particles, which is transliterated as *men,* is always the second word of the first, *x* part of a sentence, and the second, which is rendered as *de,* is always the second word of the second, *y* clause. When you're a beginning Greek student, you're told to translate the first of these as "on the one hand," and the second as "on the other," but each, by itself, means nothing, really; they merely add flavor and structure to a sentence.

This syntactic tic gives the language a lulling, seesaw rhythm when you read it. The Greeks *men* pushed on; the Trojans *de* resisted; *ouranía men Aphroditê . . . pandêmos de Aphroditê;* the dark-haired boy, *men,* immigrant and eager; the fair-haired boy, *de,* emigrant and afraid. Plato writes: *mias* men *oun ousês heis an ên Erôs; epei de dê duo eston . . .* "If there were one *men* Aphrodite, there would be only one Eros; but since *de* there are, in fact, two of her . . ."

If you spend a long enough time reading Greek literature, that rhythm begins to structure your thinking about other things, too. The world *men* you were born into; the world *de* you choose to inhabit. Your Jewish *men* heritage, stern yet fertile, sexless (for you) because heterosexual, yet for the same reason procreative, proliferating, productive; your passion, *de,* for classical Greece, rich with fables that must always end the same way, the culture of perfected beauty and marmoreally self-sufficient bodies doomed always to repeat the same pleasures. Your desire *men* for love, stability, something like a family; the compulsion *de* towards pleasure, the vertiginous beauty of falling into pleasures that have no point other than their own elaborate fulfillment.

What is interesting about this peculiarity of Greek, though, is that the *men . . . de* sequence is not always necessarily oppositional. Sometimes—often—it can merely link two notions or quantities or names, connecting rather than separating, multiplying rather than dividing. "Phaedrus *men* made a speech along those lines, and afterwards *de* some others spoke as well," the narrator of Plato's *Symposium,* a dialogue about the possibilities of love, informs us. Inherent in this language, then, is an acknowledgment of the rich conflictedness of things. It is a tongue that sees how *x* and *y*, which look to be opposites, can be part of a sequence, can inhere, somehow, in a whole.

The whole can be a concept or a culture or a person. Here is something I'd never noticed before, because I'm used to reading these two words, these particles, in Greek characters: when I write these two small syllables down in Roman letters, I am starting to write my own name.

Brief encampments.

Living here, I'm used to hearing Chelsea being called a ghetto—sometimes ironically, by those who also live here, but more often derisively, by other gay men whose tone of voice is meant to suggest that their own lives are not as narrowly oriented as the lives of the men who live and eat and work out in a wholly gay enclave like Chelsea. It is, I imagine, much the same as the tone once used by assimilated bourgeois German Jews of the inhabitants of the Polish shtetls. It's a tone of voice I myself can't help using. I also am made uncomfortable by, am embarrassed by, the word ghetto.

"Ghetto," when used of Chelsea, seems wrong for two reasons. (And even here, in trying to articulate this error, I find that I can't help reverting to the *men* and *de* of my own identity.) For one thing, the word brings to mind whole histories of oppression, of varying degrees. It suggests very specific kinds of urban spaces that have arisen under very specific social and political and historical circumstances: spaces carved out of the body of the city in order to contain, in both senses of that word, distinct and suspect subcultures. Sometimes these surgeries seem to have been conducted by the mutual if also mutually suspicious consent of both the oppressive overculture and the oppressed subculture; sometimes not. There is medieval Venice, with its restricted yet thriving population of Jews inhabiting the district called Gheto, a rotten-smelling place where I walked once with a slender Italian who, after sex, would tell stories so detailed that you felt they had to have been lies, stories about his ancient family whose coat of arms you could see carved into the damp stones of certain palazzi, and as he walked with me, his face as smooth and superior as a well-bred dog's, his hand occasionally brushing my backside as he leaned over to make some important point, he spoke with the detached, slightly bored authority of tour guides about the Jews of Venice, *gli ebrei come te,* Jews like you, separate, yes it is true, but they did okay also, no? And there is, say, San Francisco, another city of water, swollen after the Second World War with its wartime traffic of gay men and lesbians away from home for the first time and eager not to return to the quiet tree-lined spaces they had come from, eager to stay here, where there were others like them, however imperfect their freedoms might be. There are these places, with their cramped yet flourishing enclaves, their ghettos; and then there is Lodz. And there is Bolechów, the place my mother's family, the first family of the town, handsome, successful people, prosperous and a little vain, lived for five hundred years; the place her father left clutching a ticket his sister had paid for with her own body, a small place which briefly had its own small ghetto, after the Germans arrived in 1941, a place where there are no longer any Jews: none. We must be precise. As I sit here musing about the nuances of "ghetto" as metaphor, it occurs to me that, if the histories my grandfather told me are true, I would likely have died in a real ghetto, had my beautiful great-aunt not consented to be a bride, only to become a bride of death.

But Chelsea is different even from San Francisco's Castro district, its ghetto. Chelsea came into being in the mid-1980s not as a safe haven in which gay men might take shelter, but, if anything, to accommodate the overflowing population of a new and newly confident generation of out, middle-class gay men now too numerous for the spaces traditionally reserved for them. And so if its transformation from a desolate array of industrial lofts and low-rent housing into a bustling, culturally distinct enclave has an earlier, European model, it isn't the medieval Venetian Gheto, let alone its later, more terrible namesakes in this century, but rather the colonies of the ancient Greek city-states. "Colony" is a word that was to acquire its own evil history, of course; but it began fairly innocuously. The restless body-loving Greeks solved their own perennial overpopulation problems by sending out their more vigorous citizens to settle hitherto unknown outposts of the map. They called these places *apoikiai,* "away-from-homes." The colony is a place to be associated with expansion and, hence, success—as opposed to the ghetto, which we associate with oppression and compression and, eventually, death. The etymology of the word colony is in fact Roman rather than Greek: the Latin *colonia* owes its name to the *coloni,* the enterprising farmers who were the first colonists. The closest Greek comes is *kolonê,* which means a hill, or a grave mound.

But the real reason I want to resist thinking of where I live as a ghetto, a vital center rather than a shimmering edge, has to do more with the conflictedness, the *men* and the *de,* of things.

Recently, while I was on-line in a gay chat room, a man I'd been chatting up asked me where I lived; since he was someone whose on-line profile and picture I'd happened to like very much, I gave him my address. In a moment a small message box appeared at the corner of my screen. He'd written:

> thats not really chelsea. chelsea ends at 23 st
> above 23rd it become clinton u r really nowhere

A few hours later, after he'd left my apartment, I realized I was savoring this bit of geographical trivia—this new knowledge that I live slightly *outside* the boundaries of Chelsea; that I was, once more, on the edge, even when I thought I'd arrived at the center. For this information satisfied a sense of myself that had been crucial to my identity for as long as I could remember: the part of me that found erotic and intellectual pleasure in the sense that I myself was never wholly in a thing or place or experience, that even as I did and was and lived, there was a part of me I kept in reserve, a space that allowed me a vantage point. I imagine that it is a sense that most writers and artists are likely to tell you they have; but I now realize that I'd always thought of this sense as the thing that made me *gay*.

At the very moment I was able to articulate this, I wondered whether the very idea of a gay place—the place I and so many others had fantasized about, immigrated to—was not also structured around a series of irreconcilable conflicts, was not something founded on a paradox as odd as the one that locates the pleasure of things in the losing of them. What else do you call a place that must somehow be both an edge and a center, somewhere you could simultaneously feel utterly different, as you knew you were, yet wholly normal, as you wanted to be? A place whose inhabitants would, like you, be everything—special, distinct, rarefied, élite—that you'd always had to believe you really were in order to defend yourself against the insidious sense that you were somehow defective; yet at the same time a place where those marvelous people would seem utterly unexceptional? This place would be a paradox. And here again, Greek, the language of one of my geographies, serves best: *para,* against, *doxa,* expectation. As when, for example, opposites miraculously inhere; the odd symbiosis between things you thought were opposites.

"Topos," the word used to describe certain stock concepts and phrases deployed in both literature and politics, is a Greek word that actually means "place"—the point being that we return to familiar turns of phrase and habits of thought with as much relief as we return to our own homes, or neighborhoods. These days, there are topoi of gay rhetoric as clearly identifiable as the streets of Chelsea. For example, the appeal to the needs of the "gay community" is by now a familiar topos of gay politics; just as the idea that Freud's "narcissistic" model of male homosexuality is inaccurate, because it is informed by heterosexist assumptions, has become a new topos of the new gay psychology. To me, wandering as I do between the two geographies of my own life, the most interesting and yet always suspect topos in the ongoing debate about gay culture and identity is that there is such a thing as "gay identity" at all. A few years ago I was asked to review together two books about gay culture that represented, in a way, the *men* and *de* of current thinking on this subject. One, by Urvashi Vaid, once fêted at Chelsea's Barracuda bar, where you never see women, assumes, for its arguments, that being gay and being "queer"—radically and irreducibly different—are the same thing; the other, by Andrew Sullivan, whom I've seen now and then at FoodBar and who has posed shirtless on the cover of *Poz* magazine, ultimately suggests that gay men are "virtually normal"—identical to their straight brothers save for the discrete, and one supposes discreet, matter of sexual-object choice. (One example of such an object choice would be shirtless young men, presumably.) Each has constructed an appropriate politics: Vaid advocates revolution, a total reconstruction of politics that would not merely tolerate but embrace queerness; Sullivan explains why gays ought to have the legal right to marriage.

If you move from the figurative topos to a literal one— Chelsea, say—you quickly see conflict and paradox at work. The place, like the culture, hovers between identities: between the values of the heterosexual world we are all born into and those of the new gay world to which we migrated; between bourgeois convention and libidinous self-indulgence, heavenly Aphrodite and the Aphrodite of the streets; between the conservative and the radical, the banal and the exquisite, the center and the edge. Paradox is the low buzz beneath the talk you overhear at FoodBar: We are oppressed, we are fabulous; we demand equal rights, we despise the mainstream; we are men, we dress as "boys"; we talk compulsively about our desire for love, while just as compulsively we sculpt ourselves into objects suited only for desire. It's not that Vaid is right and Sullivan is wrong, or vice versa; it's that each is always only telling half the story. We're always two things at once.

And in this we are not so different from many others in a long series of ghettoized cultures and peoples: Jews, Italians, blacks, Poles, Greeks, Puerto Ricans. The list is infinite because all Americans are, in the end, inauthentic, something else, something multiple and hybrid. All these cultures and peoples have found themselves faced with the same riddle: How do you know who you are? Balanced on the fulcrum that is that hyphen (African-American, Jewish-American, Italian-American), which part of you weighs more? If you smooth

yourself out, fit in, assimilate (if you can), do you lose something vital, something definitive? If you remain outside, cling
fiercely to that core, are you solipsistic, provincial, immature?
Can balance be maintained? The idea that gay culture, or any
culture, could ever be a single coherent thing had to be a myth,
in the end, because these hyphenated identities themselves
belong to the realm of the mythic. Myth, after all, is the
domain of the strange hybrid—the centaur or the sphinx,
creatures that are two things at once, aberrations whose very
nature forces you, ultimately, to consider the question of who
you yourself—you who present to the eyes of others the
appearance of a beautiful whole, the flawless marble athlete
binding his hair, *diadoumenos*—might really be. The Greeks,
who seemed to have devoted their myths equally to perfect
beauty and to terrible corporeal bifurcation, knew that identity
is not an answer—the optimistic, American fallacy—but the
riddle itself. What is the thing that has four legs at morning and
two at noon and three in the evening? the man-eating Sphinx
asked all those entering and leaving the small space that was
Thebes; and only Oedipus, who was, catastrophically, too
many things at once to too many people, intuited that all these
things were one. *A human being,* he answered, arrogant in his
cleverness, *who crawls in infancy, walks erect in adulthood, and leans
on a cane in old age.* Only multiplex Oedipus knew that a single
person could be many secret things at the same time. (Not
everyone in Oedipus's story was as eager as he for self-
knowledge. "God spare you the knowledge of your own
birth!" his wife-mother, Jocasta, cries in Sophocles' *Oedipus the
King.*) Greek grammar, unlike most others, unlike Latin, the
language of the practical Romans, has a special verbal mode
called "the middle voice," which is neither active nor passive
but, in a way, both at once: a voice in which the subject of the

verb is also its object. *Diadoumenos,* for example, is a participle in the middle voice: *the one binding his head/whose head is being bound,* the beautiful boy who ties a ribbon around his own head/around whose head a ribbon is being tied, adorning and adorned, subject and object. Identity, the Greeks knew, is a paradox.

Gay identity, as we actually experience it, so many of us who live here, is, in the end, nothing if not structured by paradox and conflict, by the mysteries of *men* and *de.* You can be two things at once; you can live in the middle voice. You can, some of us have learned, be "queer" and "mainstream" at the same time, someone equally committed to your family in the suburbs, *men,* and to the pleasures of random encounters with strange men in the city, *de;* someone who argues eloquently for equal rights but insists on living in an all-gay, all-male enclave; someone who desires love but also loves desire. This is why I can't be satisfied by living in the place I'd dreamed about when I was seventeen and almost wasted away that year when I finally revealed myself to the shiny-haired swimmer I had silently loved for four years and he fled, refusing to speak to me ever again, so that I fled in turn, ran from home one autumn day, wandered the streets apparently aimlessly, though of course I ended up in the other side of town, where he lived, the fancy neighborhood that was jokingly called—because of its preponderance of prosperous Jews, people who would not let their children apply to pagan, Southern schools—the Golden Ghetto; and there I paced back and forth along his street, as though the intensity of my desire for him would make something happen, make him appear, but of course he didn't. And when he didn't, I went home, grew ill and depressed, couldn't eat, cried all the time, mystifying and angering my frightened parents, and thought briefly, shallowly, adolescently, of dying. But haunted even then by the specter of further, future possibilities, of course I lived. This, ultimately, is why I fled here, to this ghetto, where in the end someone will always take you. This is the place where I decided to live, the place of paradox and hybrids. The place that, in the moment of choosing it, taught me that wherever I am is the wrong place for half of me.

The most complete version of the myth of Narcissus is to be found in the *Metamorphoses,* a first-century A.D. epic poem by Ovid, a Roman who loved Greek culture. Ovid was exiled at the height of his career by the emperor Augustus—the Ronald Reagan of his day, a shrewd man who understood that the rhetoric of family values was a more effective political tool than elections or even armies—for a reason that remains a mystery even now. The only hint we have is from the poet himself, who in an abject series of verse letters to the stony and unforgiving emperor mentions his *carmen et error,* "a poem and a mistake." The consensus among scholars has long been that both the poem and the mistake were erotic in nature. When I first read the *Metamorphoses,* during the same autumn term that saw my errand in the cemetery and hence before I could name what it was I wanted, I wondered what error of desire can be so terrible that it drives you permanently away from home, from the place that, at least to begin with, defined who you were.

The myth that Ovid tells, weaving together, in turn, the myths that he had heard and read, fashioning them into what we think of as the definitive version, is by now familiar. Narcissus, a beautiful youth, falls hopelessly in love with his own reflection after stopping to take a drink in a cool glade.

Entranced by the alluring image that he takes to be a water sprite, he is constantly thwarted in his attempts to make contact: whenever he leans forward to clasp the neck he sees there, he touches only insubstantial water; when he speaks lovingly to the marmoreally white face, with its eyes like twin stars, the lips he desires also move, but utter no clear speech. After days of hopeless pining, he wastes away and dies. "Death," Ovid writes, "closed the eyes that had marveled at their owner's beauty."

I will come back to Narcissus, to boys absorbed in mirrors; but for now I want only to note two small details.

The first is that the Narcissus myth in Ovid is in fact the second half of a more complete story. The first half relates how, before he ever had the bad luck to see himself, beautiful Narcissus taunted a nymph called Echo, who had loved the boy from afar for a long while. Echo lived under a terrible curse, a punishment for a tendency to chatter: she could only repeat what others said. One day, while hunting in a dense forest, Narcissus became separated from his companions. "Is anyone here?" he yelled; and Echo, concealing herself, could only cry back, "Here!" Curious, Narcissus called for the hidden stranger to come. "Come!" Echo called back. And so on. Finally Narcissus said, "Let us meet," words that Echo happily . . . well, echoed. But when she revealed herself, Narcissus was horrified, and shunned her. A stricken Echo wasted away with longing; the only thing that remains of her is, as we know, her voice. Ovid does not specify why Narcissus was horrified by the sight of Echo; but he does tell us that his subsequent fatal enrapturement with his own pretty face was a punishment. Not for the fate of Echo, as it happens, but for his even earlier ill treatment of a male suitor, whom Ovid does

not name. This man had pursued Narcissus, but the youth cru-
elly rejected him. These things, at least, do not change. Embit-
tered, the man called down curses on the beautiful youth's
head.

Ovid was a Roman, not a Greek; but there is no doubt that
he spoke Greek, and if, like Ovid, you are a foreigner in love
with Greek, if you know Greek, it is difficult to resist the
notion that he purposely wove the paradox of *men* and *de* into
his story. For the story of Echo is nothing if not a story about
difference mistaken for sameness: in it, the object and subject
are in fact discrete, two separate individuals but (at least ini-
tially) seem to be indistinguishable; and the story of Narcissus,
as we know, is a story about sameness mistaken for difference,
in which the object and subject are in fact the same but seem
to be different, two different beings. Recently, gay psychology
has become wary of Narcissus and his myth as a means to
explain the male homosexual psyche; it is thought that the narcissistic model of male homosexuality is unfair, heterosexist,
that it puts gay desire in an unfavorable, biased light. This may
be so. Still, taken together, both Echo and Narcissus may, in a
very different way, be useful in explaining the paradoxical state
of gay culture as a whole—explaining why it may be more
authentic, ultimately, to spend your life wandering between
two geographies than to pretend you can live in only one. For
queer ideology is a kind of Narcissus's tale, in which an important sameness keeps getting overlooked because of an insistence that there is only difference; while the "assimilationist"
creed reminds you of Echo's story, in which a crucial, perhaps
irreducible difference gets covered over by an apparent sameness, a voice that seemed to be saying, "I am you, I am you, I
am you."

The juxtaposition of the two suggests that Ovid, at least, thought the truth of human identity lingered somewhere between the two: the *men* of total polarity, the *de* of ostensible sameness. All in all, it is not a bad conclusion to have come to, satisfyingly complex and very humane—though of course it did not save Ovid, who ended his life in a provincial Black Sea backwater called Tomis, to which a vindictive Augustus had sent the urbane sophisticate, knowing full well that he'd wither and die there as inevitably as did Echo and Narcissus. (Bland, cultureless Tomis wasn't all that different, in its way, from the hinterlands from which so many gay men flee to the ghettos.) And indeed, Ovid's delicately constructed balances haven't proved very appealing to those who are writing about gay culture or arguing about gay politics, who instead have tended to posit a single, monolithic entity called "gay identity" in order to make their arguments work: "queer," "gay," "mainstream," whatever. It's not hard to see the reason: you cannot have identity politics or polemics, after all, unless you have a recognizable identity. But when measured against the dense complexities of lived experience, that reading of "identity" can't help seeming inadequate—more useful than true; flat, easy, safe. The image the water reflects isn't always the complaisant one we want; the truth is richer, more complex, more satisfying.

And, to be sure, more problematic. For a man to dream that he saw himself reflected in water was, the Greeks thought, a premonition of his own death. Knowledge—a clear vision of your own image—can be dangerous. Knowledge may make you aware that the certainties of others are often more convenient than true, allowing those who hold them to live a coherent and sensible life, allowing their choices and their ideologies to make a kind of sense. Knowledge of the complexities, of the *men* and *de* of things, will destabilize you, fragment your sense of who you are, shatter your identity.

Which brings me to my second detail. We are told that Narcissus's mother, a nymph, once asked the blind prophet Tiresias (among whose mythic accomplishments could be counted the feat of having lived as both a male and a female, and who thus was the living embodiment of *men* and *de*) whether the child would live to old age. In Ovid, the nymph consults the ancient seer just after she has given birth to her son; but in another version, a version my Venetian friend insisted on, a version I much prefer—for are not prophecy and pregnancy alike, two conditions in which you are filled with the future?—Narcissus's mother approaches the old prophet just before she is due, when she is still huge with the child within her.

In this version, the girl is seeking knowledge, wanting to know whether her unborn child will have a good life. The weary old man stands there, exhausted with all his knowledge, his skin as supple and tough as old leather, his hands gnarled, frightening the girl, perhaps, with the filmy, albumin-streaked eyes that, within themselves, in the dark of the brain, see everything. What do they see? They see the beautiful girl who is standing in front of him, her upper lip damp with fear; they see the skin beneath her gauzy gown stretched shiny and tight over the huge belly that is ready to burst, like a fruit, grown so big that the crescent of pubic hair has disappeared, down, down, where only his blind eyes can see it; they see the fetus grown to term within the belly, and, beyond that, like the seed within the stone within the fruit, the beautiful boy, long-limbed, who is already lying within the fetus that lies clenched within the tired misshapen girl. And they can see, finally, as the old man peers with his special vision of what comes later, they can see the boy trying to embrace what he sees in the water; the seer can see the tips of his curls—dark? blond? we do not know—wet with the pond; he can see the boy's own vision blurring as his face nears the water, all distinctions already rippling into nothingness: the old man can see all this, and he already knows, as the boy does not and cannot ever know, that what the boy is looking for is not there, that the embrace he seeks must always elude him, that there is nothing between the lips and the water, between the desire and the reflection, only the myth and the mirror, only unfulfillable desire, and madness, and extinction.

Yes, the old man finally says—this part is in both versions, Ovid's and mine—yes, he says, shaking himself alert, blinking his blind eyes back to the present: a blind man trying not to see—a paradox—the old man trying to keep the girl from trying to know the mystery of identity; a hopeless task, as he already knows. Yes, the unborn child might yet live to an old age: *Si se non noverit.* "Only if he never knows himself."

II. MULTIPLICITIES

The English noun *identity* comes, ultimately, from the Latin adverb *identidem*, which means "repeatedly." The Latin has exactly the same rhythm as the English, buh-BUM-buh-BUM—a simple iamb, repeated; and *identidem* is, in fact, nothing more than a reduplication of the word *idem*, "the same": *idem(et)idem. Same (and) same.* The same, repeated. It is a word that does exactly what it means.

It seems odd, at first glance, that a noun that we associate with distinctiveness and individuality, with the irreducible uniqueness of each person, should derive from one that denotes (and even sounds like) nothing but mechanical repetition. But once you've given it some thought, the etymology of *identity* makes a kind of sense. At least one way of establishing what something is, after all, is to see whether it always remains itself, and nothing else, over and over again. This is also the case, presumably, for people: you are, endlessly and repeatedly, *you,* and not some other.

On the etymological model, at least, identity sounds like a reassuring thing.

A young boy of nine or ten is standing in front of a mirror. It is late morning on a school day, in winter; the house is filled with cool indifferent light. The boy is hoping he is ill.

The mirror is the only full-length mirror in his parents' house, and it hangs in their smallish bedroom. Although not technically off-limits, this was not somewhere his parents' children would normally idle during the day. It's a place, instead, where they might go at night, to ask their father to help with their math homework—he's a mathematician, and answers their questions with a crisp, professional impatience, mildly incredulous at their inability to understand what to him seems so natural—or, more likely, where they might go in the late afternoon, after school, hauling loads of laundry hot from the dryer for their mother to fold, since she has convinced herself, and by now her children as well, that only she knows how to fold the laundry in the correct way, and does so day after day, sitting on the floor with her right leg propped up on the bed, the leg that is trellised with varicose veins, some as thick as worms, others as delicate as creepers, the whole clotted limb wrapped round with elastic bandages that make it look fake. She sits there with her bad leg propped on the bed and watches the Million Dollar Movie and sometimes cries, and it's hard for this boy, her second son, to tell whether she's weeping for a character called Jane Eyre ("foolish Jane," Rochester says, powerful and condescending in the knowledge that he is desired), so long invisible to her tyrannical and silent master, or for the fact, which the boy already senses even if he cannot articulate it, that this woman's own silent husband turned out to be so confusingly unlike her tyrannical father. Perhaps, he thinks, she is weeping for her own mother, his soft grandmother who died a few years ago, the biggest event so far, he thinks, in the life of his family; maybe it is she whom his mother cries for, his grandmother, dead swiftly and unexpectedly a month past her fifty-ninth birthday, a woman who bore in silence and sometimes in fear the tyrannies and condescensions of the glamorous and authoritative husband who thought her foolish and who outlived her.

This is the room where the mirror hangs, next to the headboard of the bed that the mathematician and his wife have slept in for fifteen years. The other mirrors in the house—there were only two, much wider than tall—are in the bathrooms, and hang above the shallow sinks; but they afford only head-and-shoulders views, once you'd grown tall enough to see yourself in them, and so if you want to see all of yourself at once, see what you look like to other people, you have to go into their room, the room where the air is heavy with the math questions you are too embarrassed to ask and the floor has been reduced to the alleys between teetering ziggurats of hot white towels. Here is where you go to tie your tie or size up the impact of your outfits, or, more secretly, to look at your own face, which is what this boy is doing now, on a winter's morning in, say, 1969.

It is not the first time he has stood in front of this narrow oblong, staring at himself. He often sneaks in here in the quiet afternoons, sometimes to get away from his siblings—of whom there are many but who are unlikely to come in here and find him; he relishes being alone and often hides in the basement or in the crabapple tree just to get away from the noise of these brothers and the sister—but mostly just to look at himself. Sometimes he merely stares; sometimes he plays with his own features, twisting and mashing them as if to see whether he will still be himself, still have the same thoughts and hear the same voices in his head despite the violence to the face that, for as long as he can remember, has been described to him, at least by his mother's family, as a handsome one, pretty, *shayn*. At other times he has discovered that, if he takes his mother's hand mirror and holds it behind his head while looking in this mirror, an infinitely long corridor, filled with nothing but him, opens out in front of and behind him. He loves to do this. He often plays with the two mirrors, the one in his hand and the one on the wall, tilting the smaller one this way and that in order to change the part of himself that is being endlessly reflected in the larger one: the crown of his head, his thin neck, his chin, his hair, and, of course, his face, which is the face of his mother's family, of his mother's mother but also of his mother's aunts, beautiful dead girls.

When the boy gazes into the mirror it is different from when the mathematician stands there, absently tying one of his many almost identical ties. Sometimes the boy will watch in secret from the door of his parents' bedroom as his father dresses himself. With a rapid efficient flurry of hands and fabric, the mathematician, arms akimbo, elbows moving, finishes his tie and then moves away from the mirror towards the door frowning, thinking and sometimes talking to himself of something else. The boy compares this brusque morning ritual unfavorably with the exacting toilette of his grandfather, his mother's still handsome father, a compact man with a largish head who, on those occasions when he comes to visit—with his many suitcases and whichever of his many wives he happens to be married to at that moment, with his attaché case filled with orange and blue and green pills, with his filter-tip cigars and his pet canary whose name is Schloimele, Yiddish for Solomon, his grandfather's favorite biblical character, another man with many wives—dresses himself with a fastidious self-absorption so complete that it goes beyond vanity and achieves a kind of purity.

When his mother's father dresses himself each morning, a ritual that can take three-quarters of an hour, he first lays out his clothes on a bed, the way salesclerks in fancy stores do, making a hollow mockup of a human figure, a flat man consisting of socks, pants, shirt, vest, tie; then he scrutinizes the outfit, carefully removing to one side anything that doesn't strike him as right (a pair of socks, for instance, that is not quite the right shade of mustard) and replacing it with something better, something perfect. Fresh from his bath, the old man stands in his knee-length undershorts and splashes some cologne on, slaps some witch hazel on the back of his neck, and then begins dressing. First he puts on his socks—*Socks before pants,* he tells his grandson, as if this is something very important, *that way you don't ruin the crease in your pants bending over to pull them up*—and then hoists up his trousers and then pulls on a T-shirt, covering the soft white-haired torso with its many scars ("This one I got fighting Pocahontas's tribe," he will say, pointing to a long red furrow that almost bisects his chest) and, the boy has noticed, its one nipple; then he steps carefully into the starched shirt and, perhaps, a tie, and if not a tie then a thin woolen vest or cardigan, even in summer; and finally the shoes, always beautifully polished, which he puts on only after he has carefully hoisted up the trouser leg at the knee and placed the small foot up on a chair. Then he smooths the sides of his head with a few strokes of a flat rectangular tortoiseshell brush—he has white hair there, and a few strands down the middle, too, which he also brushes—and, when all this is done, he brushes himself off with his flat, square, hairy hands, removing any offending pieces of lint, or maybe a stray hair. Only then will he turn and say to the boy, "Now we can go out."

So this is the old man's routine, precise, formal, exacting, so different from the way the boy's father dresses. At this point in his life, the boy prefers his grandfather.

When the boy looks at himself in the mirror in his parents' bedroom it is also different from his mother's careful inspection of her face in her magnifying mirror, which she will sometimes set up on the kitchen table before she has to go out at night, gossiping with her children when she can get them to stay there or, more often, watching an old movie on the tiny television the mathematician bought for her to watch during 2 a.m. feedings after the last child, a girl, was born. When she prepares to go out, the boy's mother sits at the wooden trestle table in the kitchen and, like a surgeon (he thinks), lays out her instruments on one of the spotless white towels she has so meticulously folded: a small white china bowl of sudsy water, raspy emery boards, shiny pointed steel things for her nails, cotton balls, makeup, things whose purpose the boy cannot identify and the names of which he does not know, things to curl her eyelashes, things to smooth her eyebrows, which like his are shaped exactly like a circumflex, the accent the French call a *chapeau,* a hat. As she works on her face she scrutinizes it with the unsentimental intensity of a painter sizing up a blank canvas. Often she will pull her face into grotesque elongated shapes, making a big oval O with her mouth, or opening her blue-gray eyes unnaturally wide, in exaggerated, silent-movie astonishment, the better to appraise some detail of lipstick or mascara that needs seeing to. She seems not to notice the comic absurdity of these grimaces, which make her son giggle softly as he watches her. Because she has been beautiful her whole life, she can afford to be unsentimental about her face.

So these are his parents: the father, the mathematician, who has always been oblivious to the mirror and what it tells him (he still asks his wife what to wear each morning); the mother, a schoolteacher, who relies on it, scrutinizes the image it throws back at her in order to become herself each day. But for the boy the mirror is something else altogether. He never thinks of what he sees there as a surface, but rather as something more like a door, as though the boy who stares back at him from the mirror's surface is in fact *behind it,* somewhere else, someplace that has its own depth, its own reality.

On this day in 1969, the boy is neither purposefully distorting nor idly exulting in his own image, but instead is looking for something specific. For a week his older brother has had chicken pox, and because the boy is jealous of the attention the brother is getting, he's asked his brother to breathe on him, so that he too might become sick, the object of attention, important. Now, on this morning when the boy has begun to run a high fever—he doesn't need to hold the thermometer up to the high-wattage light bulb in the reading lamp that is screwed into the wall above his bed, the way he does when he wants to stay home from school—on this morning he is staring in the mirror, and notes with huge satisfaction that while his face is still clear, there are three red marks on his torso. He runs his fingers over them: they're shiny and swollen like pimples, and they provoke an urge to pop them.

His mother, who is in the kitchen folding more laundry, is watching an old movie on the tiny television set and (he imagines, because he knows her habits well) copying over on a fresh sheet of lined paper, with her red Flair pen, a list of the times the older brother has taken his medication—as if changing the paper on which lists are written were an established medical procedure with proven therapeutic value, like changing dressings, or sheets.

The boy has been staring so long at his face that it begins to break up, losing its coherence, devolving into a meaningless collection of bumps and hollows, of shiny bits and of odd furry bits. He has been thinking this: how funny your eyebrows look once you stop thinking of them as eyebrows—as *eyebrows*—and start to see them as random collections of hair streaked above your eyes, like animal tracks, like something forgotten or unfinished. Deprived of context, they cease to be recognizably themselves and become a little disturbing, as though they shouldn't be on your face . . .

This boy's face is burning. He presses the flesh around his mouth and eyes with cool fingers. As he turns away from the mirror, he faints.

Opposite the mirror, directly behind him and to his right, against the wall of his parents' bedroom, is his mother's Moderne dresser, a sleek teak thing dutifully oiled each Tuesday by his mother's Polish cleaning lady, a solid woman who still wears her thick dark hair the way she probably wore it in the forties, when she was a strong young woman working on a farm not too far from the town where the boy's grandfather was born, and where his grandfather's brother lived and prospered and then was killed; a woman to whom the boy's grandfather, when he comes, likes to tell dirty jokes in Polish, while she delightedly pretends to be shocked. Each Tuesday afternoon this powerful woman carefully rubs oil into the massive dresser, following dutifully if somewhat skeptically the instructions the boy's mother has given her; the Polish woman is by now used to the exigencies, grown of boredom or desperation or minor madness, of the *pani,* the comfortable upper-middle-class Jewish ladies for whom she works. It is on the sharp corner of this gleaming demonstration of his mother's zeal for order and cleanliness that the boy hits his head as he falls to the floor, woozy with the fever, or perhaps with the effort of staring at himself for so long. The dresser, rather than the fever, is what causes the boy to remain unconscious for some time.

When he comes to, he cannot remember who he is.

This was not as bad as you might think. When the boy finally opens his eyes, he looks around, sees a ceiling but does not know what room it belongs to, sees walls hung with pictures that are unfamiliar to him. Against one wall there is a long, low, gleaming dresser; on the floor on which he is sprawled, his legs pointing towards a narrow mirror on another wall, a golden carpet spreads out, as impersonal as something in a hotel. Everything is strange—not odd, but merely unknown, a strangeness that evokes nothing more than indifference, evokes no more emotion than if the man this boy has by now become were to find himself in the wrong aisle of a mall parking lot. You will wonder whether this boy tried to ask himself where he was, but of course this was impossible, because the "I" that has to be the subject of any such questioning was equally a mystery. He knows he must have a name, and tries to think what it could be, not urgently, not in panic, but the way you might try to reconstruct a shopping list you'd left at home—important, but not, in the end, urgent. This doesn't work. After a while he wants to call out the name of someone who might help him, but he doesn't know whose name to call. It occurs to him that he might live here alone, but this seems unreasonable because it's clear he's only a boy, must have a mother, a father. Finally he heeds the mirror and sits up, imagining that once he sees himself he'll remember who he is.

No. He stands up and sees a hand mirror on the dresser. He picks it up; the endless corridor opens up. But even that shows him nothing helpful.

It isn't until he hears his mother's voice, calling out for him from where she sits in the kitchen with her lists or her hot towels or whatever it is that she is doing, that he is jolted into memory, remembers who he is. But in that small time, before he becomes filled up again with himself, he feels something like elation. Everything is clearly amiss, and yet he senses that it will come right again—just as his features had, in the end, reassembled themselves into something recognizable, so would the rest of him. In the meanwhile: how delicious to play hooky from yourself. It can make you giddy, this staring into a corridor of mirrors and not knowing the identity of any of the infinity of boys who can, after all, do nothing but look back at you.

One of the greatest and most authoritative love lyrics in the Western canon was actually written twice. It was first composed by Sappho, notoriously a resident of the island called Lesbos, in about 600 B.C., in a dialect of Greek. This we know because the entire poem, which is called "Sappho 31" because it appears thirty-first in the traditional listing of Sappho's lyrics, comes down to us as a quotation: the poem is cited in a much later ancient text, a volume of literary criticism called *On the Sublime,* attributed—probably wrongly—to someone called Longinus, writing around the time of Christ. Already in antiquity, then, the poem was established as a canonical expression of desire.

Yet for us the lyric is perhaps more familiar in the Latin translation, learned by generations of secondary school and college Latin students, that was made by the young Roman poet Catullus, born in about 84 B.C. and dead not quite thirty years later—a translation so charged with that later poet's personality that it is, ultimately, less a translation than an adaptation. Like Sappho's, Catullus's poem has no name. Classicists refer to it simply as "Catullus 51," because it appears fifty-first in the traditional listing of *his* poems; but it is sometimes difficult not to imagine that the intensity and excess of the poem's emotions, compressed in five neat four-line stanzas, make a title superfluous.

People always refer to Catullus 51 as a love poem, but it is just as much a poem about looking. In it, the poet-narrator describes the effects of seeing someone *else* looking at and talking to the object of his own erotic passion. Within the poem, the narrator watches this strange man talking to his girlfriend (*her* girlfriend, in the original); but the poem as a whole constitutes a frame within which you, the reader, can observe the poet-lover, suffering. Reading it is like entering a hall of mirrors.

One way to translate Sappho's first stanza would be:

> He seems to me to be equal to the gods—
> the man who, sitting just across from you,
> speaking sweet words softly in your ear,
>   waits for an answer.

Catullus, a hot-blooded Veronese, clearly feels the need to one-up his female predecessor in his translation of these lines. The man who to Sappho "seems equal to the gods" becomes, in Catullus's much later version, a man who "seems to *surpass* the gods." Why is this man, observed by the poet, so special, powerful? Because he is able not only to contemplate but also to *talk to* the object of his passion, an object that the tongue-tied poet-observer-narrator can only watch, her/his heart aching, ears ringing, eyesight fading, breath coming shorter and shorter. Among other things, the poem is a catalogue of the symptoms of frustrated desire. Here is Catullus:

> *ille mi par esse deo videtur—*
> *ille, si fas est, superare divos*
> *qui sedens adversus identidem te*
> *spectat et audit . . .*

> That man seems to me to be like a god—
> seems (if it is not blasphemy to say so) to surpass
> the gods—
> the man who, sitting opposite you, again and again
> watches and hears you . . .

Superare divos, "surpass the gods," is, in part, a young man's excess. But the later poet's use of "surpass" is, also, something of an in-joke: you can't help thinking that it refers as much to Catullus's relation to Sappho as it does to the nameless man's ("that man"'s) relation to the gods whom he supposedly surpasses.

I was made to memorize this poem in a Latin poetry class in the fall of 1979, when I was nineteen and couldn't focus my eyes on the brown-and-yellow hardback textbook because of the paleness of the hair of the boy who sat across the room from me: a strange, lunar color, not at all like the rich straw I'd become familiar with from furtive observation of the blond, smiling students around me.

The poem's not difficult to memorize. This is partly because of its meter, an insinuating and repetitive chain of

long strokes and short gasps, and partly because of the asso-
nances that link its component words and lines: the first line is
composed of the same sequence of vowel sounds that com-
prise the second—*ih-eh-ee-ah-eh*—as if the lover's obsessive-
ness, his need to relive and reconstitute the experience of
being with the object, were being reproduced even at the most
primal, inarticulate level of his utterances, *ih-eh-ee-ah-eh* . . .
This is how babies talk, seeking mastery through repetition.
Much later on, I would see this myself, in a child I know well;
but then, when I was a sophomore in college, the point was
made, with restrained self-congratulation, by our Latin professor, an ancient man whose life's work was a reference work
about a reference work about Vergil, a small stalagmite of
scholarship built up over decades in tiny accretions. This man
was in his seventies and wore bowties; his hair was disconcert-
ingly, unnaturally dark. From beneath this shiny, black, bril-
liantined helmet he would tell us things about Roman poetry,
things that must have filtered into my consciousness even as I
secretly watched the moon-haired boy across the room.

I had seen this boy before. He'd been in another class with
me the previous spring and had, notoriously, fallen asleep during a seminar session dedicated to Euripides' *Ion,* a play about a
boy with two fathers. Since I'd been watching him in that class,
too, I saw it happening, saw him falling asleep that day, and was
torn between disdain for his indifference to the subject, *my*
subject, and a kind of amazed elation that anyone could live so
thoroughly outside the elaborate web of inhibitions and sensi-
tivities that organized my own reactions to the world that he
didn't care if he just fell asleep in class. So I watched as the
blond head bobbed downwards—a movement interrupted, as
with a toy on a string, by tiny upward jerks—and finally came
to rest on his chest, until finally the professor, who was to

become my adviser and mentor, a small feline woman with bobbed hair who was an eminent scholar of Homer and who exhaled long spirals of cigarette smoke between sentences, said, with cruel quiet, "If we're boring you, you're more than welcome to leave," and the head jerked up and he flushed a deep red to the roots of his hair.

Even before this, I'd been watching him. He was a part-time university bus driver, and always wore the same thing when he worked: white painter's cap, white T-shirt, white overalls. When I boarded a bus and saw him there in the driver's seat, I would go to the back and allow myself to be carried along, acting as though I lived at the end of his route, which wasn't true, so that I could hold on that much longer to the sight of his pale hair beneath his white hat, the baggy shape of his white clothes, which, through a strange opposition, suggested the slender body underneath. Of course we never spoke. Sometimes other male students who were obviously his friends—they all dressed alike—would board the bus and sit there in front, across from him, talking in their rough excited voices about games and parties and dates, and he would laugh with them. His teeth were very white, like stones. I hated these other boys because I knew they did not see in him what I saw, and I thought that what I saw was better, more beautiful; yet I envied them their proximity, and so hated myself, too. When I pushed the doors open to exit the bus, it was like something snapping.

The paradox of the mirror—this is something the boy thinks of quite a bit, as he grows from ten to eleven, from eleven to twelve, from twelve into panicked adolescence—the paradox of the mirror is that although it reproduces you perfectly, the image you see is always in reverse: it is the same but also exactly opposite. If the boy were to look at a photograph of himself, he would see the beauty mark that spots his left cheekbone on the right side of the picture; this is what other people see when they see him. But this beauty mark belongs to the left side of the mirror, as if the boy in the mirror had a mark on his right cheek. Everything else is precisely the same: like certain other members of his mother's family, his right eye is slightly bigger, more open, than the left, although with the boy in the mirror it is the opposite; that boy has a scar on his forehead that zigzags to the left, not the right; and so on.

So the mirror provides a mixed pleasure. On the one hand, it creates inexhaustible multiplicities, corridors-within-corridors filled with infinitely repeating images; and yet the images it offers are doomed to fail (with a kind of stunning exactitude) to do what they are supposed to do, which is to show you what you look like.

The sameness that is also difference, the conundrum presented by the mirror, interests him. It creates in him a special appreciation of surfaces and what they might conceal.

This is especially interesting to him since the world he inhabits seems foreign and, sometimes, hostile. In it there are other boys his age, whose roughness and unself-consciousness frighten him; there is the reality of his life, which consists, at least on the outside, of going to school and being afraid of getting beaten up, and then coming home and eating fish sticks with his brothers and sister and mother while his father works late being a mathematician, a job the boy doesn't understand and which his father doesn't explain to him; there are other kids' fathers, bluff overweight men who smell of food and who carpool to the city each morning and whose jobs are, in their way, equally mysterious to him, since all he knows of what they do is that they are "in ladies' undergarments"; there is his mother, who brings armfuls of flowers from her garden to the checkout girls at the supermarket, who sometimes will call him and his brothers in from doing whatever they are doing outside to see some peonies or roses or tiny daisies she has cut from her gardens, saying, "Look at that! Look how the petals are arranged! Isn't nature *wonderful*?" and who at other times calls them in and makes them remake their beds because the hospital corners aren't at right angles. There are these things, which the boy experiences but doesn't feel part of. This is the surface of his life, and it is much flatter than the experiences he would like to have: the stories in the books he reads, or the ones that his mother's father tells, when the old man comes to this flat town that a year before the boy was born was one vast potato farm, and sits in his special chair and tells his stories.

In this broad flat suburb where the pin oaks are so recently planted that they seem artifical, the boy's grandfather is exciting because he is different, and his difference makes the boy feel special and rarefied among the other children, of whom he is afraid. He sometimes uses his strange and exciting grandfather *against* them. Once, when he is about ten, he tells a red-haired boy from the neighborhood to call for him the next day, early in the morning, when he knows his grandfather will be davening, saying his morning prayers, which his grandfather, who is Orthodox, has done every day of his life since 1915, when he turned thirteen. The neighborhood boy, who attends the local parochial school, appears as instructed, early in the morning, and when the front door opens he beholds the old man standing in the living room, immaculately dressed of course but also attired in things this Catholic boy has never laid eyes on: a huge ivory-and-blue-striped tallis around the old man's shoulders, falling nearly to the floor, and the religious tokens called phylacteries: the two black leather boxes, containing scraps of Torah written on parchment, that the old man dutifully binds each morning, with black leather bands, one to his gleaming forehead and the other to his hairy left arm. (Another morning ritual.) The boy's grandfather wears these things as he stands there muttering and swaying back and forth, murmuring prayers he has said so many thousands of times that he cannot even feel the meaning of the words any more; and when the old man sees the strange boy at the door, which his grandson has opened wide, stepping back in order to let his friend see his grandfather at prayer, he does not say anything, doesn't interrupt the discipline of his prayer, but in irritation at being interrupted merely raises the level of his Hebrew muttering so that it becomes a kind of yelling, and the red-haired boy, after taking one long look at this apparition, turns and runs. The old man turns his back to the door and continues praying.

By the time the boy is twelve he has found ways to forget about the surfaces around him. He becomes very interested in two things: archaeology, which he reads about constantly, and genealogy, which he researches doggedly, writing to relatives, interviewing his grandfathers with a tape recorder, typing (on the cast-iron Underwood typewriter that belonged to his grandfather's secretary in his passementerie factory on West Twenty-sixth Street) long letters to the Municipal Archives in downtown Manhattan, hoping to get copies of certificates of births and deaths.

Both of these backwards-looking hobbies support his greatest obsession, which is learning languages. For a long time he has listened, wide-eyed, when his mother's father comes to visit and speaks his many languages: Russian, Polish, Yiddish,

German, even Hungarian, a language the grandfather claims to have known well enough, when he was eighteen and en route to America, to get a job as a translator in the Hungarian embassy in Berlin, and yet to have forgotten so completely that, in his sixties, he cannot remember a single word. The boy's grandfather, when he comes, receives his surviving siblings and nieces and nephews and former neighbors in great state at the home of the boy's parents. These old people come from the Bronx and Brooklyn and Manhattan and Queens, from their stale-smelling apartments on Atlantic Avenue and the Grand Concourse, and sit at the boy's parents' dining room table, wearing fancy dresses or ties and jackets and pants whose top buttons they will open by the end of the meal, and at these special gatherings, at which they pay homage to the boy's grandfather, they speak in many languages, moving from one to the other as the moment and the subject dictate. The boy's grandfather tells jokes in Yiddish and then translates them into English or Russian or German or, if the cleaning woman is present, the woman who oils the sleek wooden furniture, into Polish. For the boy, sitting in a corner and watching, not daring to speak, this ability of his grandfather's to speak many languages is the most mysterious and powerful thing about the old man, who sits there in his immaculately creased trousers drinking straight whiskey out of a large crystal tumbler and smoking a narrow cigar. The boy loves the idea of being able to slide in and out of languages, depending on whom you want to impress or seduce.

For all that the boy wants to be like his grandfather, he does not want to learn Hebrew. He will eventually have to learn it, at least enough of it to read it for his bar mitzvah, which he like his three brothers will undergo not because these boys' parents are religious but because it must be done to appease their Orthodox grandfather; but Hebrew does not really interest him, it is too close to what he already knows. Everyone he knows is Jewish; Jewish is what this flat Long Island neighborhood is. Hebrew is not different enough. Already he has decided that he wants to learn the languages of the pagan Egyptians and Greeks and Romans, the oppressors of the ancient Hebrews.

Indeed, unlike those many tongues his grandfather knows, the languages the boy is eager to know are not languages that anyone speaks. Languages are, for him, private, not shared, not aural but visual, the keys to burrowing beneath surfaces, to moving backwards, more inwardly, rather than out into the world. By the time he is eleven, he has taught himself to read a few dozen Egyptian hieroglyphics, a task that is as absurd in many ways as it is difficult, since the pictures he so painstakingly memorizes each night, pictures that can stand for sounds, syllables, whole concepts, are more often than not pictures of things he has never seen: vultures and eagles and lengths of twisted hemp and seated lions and (his favorite) a human heart connected to a windpipe, a vertical that descends into an oval; it looks a bit like a banjo, but is the character for *nefer,* "beautiful." Secretly, the boy keeps a journal in which he laboriously transliterates English into these pictures. With rare exceptions, each day he writes the same thing: NOTHING IMPORTANT. By the time he is fourteen, he has learned Greek characters, which serve him better because by now more things are happening in his life, and Greek is more fluent off the pen. He still writes NOTHING IMPORTANT somewhat regularly (nu-omicron-theta-iota-nu-gamma iota-mu-pi-omicron-rho-tau-alpha-nu-tau), but he writes other things too: "I met P. today, I think we might become friends" and, about six months later, when he is suffering badly from what he does not yet recognize as love, "I refuse to believe that my idea of having a perfect friend is, as Dad says, 'shit.'" (Why is his father so crude? His father is not a crude man. It is because he is afraid—because he knows, better than his son does, what the son means when he asks about having a "perfect friend." The father's fear makes him cruel.) Because at this point the boy is more interested in alphabets than in languages, it doesn't bother him that he is writing the same language that he already knows, merely in different letters.

In the boy's bedroom hangs a framed art-postcard that shows two ancient Greek statues, cleverly photographed: in the foreground of this photograph, taking up most of the left-hand part of the image, is the large head of a statue of the Classical period, a woman's head that is slightly out of focus because the camera is focused on the statue behind. That statue, of the Archaic period, is perhaps seventy-five years older than the first, and it is a statue of two people, a woman on the left, staring straight ahead, her arms at her side, while a man stands next to her and whispers in her ear, his marble arm crooked, his stone hand cupped to her ear. Although the boy at this point doesn't think of it this way, it's a witty picture: the photographer has shot these two statues in such a way as to make it look as though the two Archaic figures in the background are whispering about the serenely beautiful Classical statue in front of them. The boy doesn't think of this picture as funny, though, because for him it is the image of his passion, of how he thinks about archaeologies and of dead writings, of the beautiful, highly structured, and intricate languages he is eager to learn, which, once you decipher them, provide exquisite but always solipsistic pleasures, because no one can hear or speak them. When he thinks of what he is doing, he thinks of that picture. He wants to hear the sound of statues speaking.

At fourteen, the boy spends most of his time alone, copying dead scripts into notebooks that only he can read and yet which he carefully buries in secret places—the shallow spaces underneath drawers, the space between his mattress and the hard bed frame that his father built—and so has no mutual experience even of puppy love; none of sex, either.

Masturbation is his only experience of the erotic. Because he cannot conceive of being able to fulfill his desires, once he knows what they are—desires that are clearly outside the bounds of normalcy, desires that involve his older brother's school friends and the boy across the street with whom this boy plays pool occasionally, and whom he tries to get to talk about sex—because he knows that his desires are for the moment unfulfillable, masturbation becomes for him something more complete, more self-sufficient, more about itself than about something else, than it probably is for most other boys his age: less anticipatory than, in its way, a fulfillment. Like the books that had paved the way for them—his first orgasm comes unprompted while he is reading a sex scene in a novel—his masturbatory fantasies are discrete, coherent, whole, unspoiled by extraneous intrusions. Even, eventually, by the intrusions of others' desire for him.

He wonders about what his classmates are doing sexually, if for no other reason than by the time he's grown to full adolescence his masturbatory life is so fevered, so constant, so complete, that he begins to see sex with other people as something of an aberration. Everything he knows about this kind of sex comes from watching, or hearing about, other teenagers, who of course are not gay, for if they were their activities would not be public enough to be observed by strangers. This boy would see people in school dating, and would wonder what it would be like to be with someone else—someone who wasn't himself. Boys he secretly dreamt of would hold the hands of their girlfriends, endure the teasing of their classmates or teammates.

Above all the boy wonders and thinks about kissing, the one thing that autoeroticism, no matter how frequent, cheats you of. He watches with interest as people kiss in movies, and carefully observes, as if he might be tested on this subject, the way they position their heads, how their jaws and throats move as they kiss. What does it look like, he wonders, when you kiss someone, as the other's face comes towards your own, until it dissolves into an unfocused blur, and your experience of it necessarily shifts, becomes one of touch and taste rather than of sight? He thinks about this a great deal, and sometimes, when he gets home from school, he goes to the mirror in his parents' room and stands just a few inches from it, bringing his face closer and closer to the mirror, closing his eyes finally so that the moment of contact is also, necessarily, a moment of blindness.

Was that it? When you made contact, you vanished?

It is odd, in a way, that Sappho 31 and Catullus 51 should be considered great love poems, since they are less about love per se than they are, as I have said, about watching; and they are less about watching, in turn, than they are about the suffering that comes from a terminally frustrated watching, a watching without consummation. "My tongue stiffens," Catullus observes (Sappho says hers *snaps*); the two poet-lovers catalogue, almost clinically, their reactions to seeing their erotic objects pursued by others. Catullus writes:

> . . . a slender flame
> seeps through my limbs; my ears ring
> with a shrill sound, my twin eyes
>   are touched by night.

Sappho goes on:

> . . . the sweat pours down me, a tremor
> seizes hold of me, I'm greener than
> grass; and it seems to me I'm just a little short
>   of dying.

Here is a desire in which the senses fail. Love, on this model, leads to a kind of death. ("A little short of dying" is the last full line of the Sapphic poem we have; only a fragment of the next stanza survives, a half-line that begins *alla pan tolmâton . . .* , "but all must be endured . . .")

A few years before I learned this lyric, watching the blond-haired bus driver in Latin class, I had been obsessively in love with another pale-headed boy, of whom this later, Southern, bus-driving boy was, I eventually realized, just a reflection. This earlier boy had come from the South, from, actually, the state where I would eventually go to college seeking him; he had come from there, a place that seemed authentic when compared with our artificial Long Island suburb, a brand-new place that betrayed its desire for authenticity, both historical and topographical, in the names it gave its streets: "Old Country," "Round Swamp." (There wasn't any swamp.) This boy seemed to all of us rather exotic: his speech was different; his manners, according to my English teacher—a woman with a carefully maintained Brahmin accent who, I know now, was watching me watching him—were better than ours; his hair was not dark, like the hair of the other students, who were almost all descendants of Sicilians and Neapolitans and Eastern European Jews. He had a normal-sounding American name that ended neither in a vowel nor in the German for "valley" or "stone" or "town." When he smiled, it was so big you could see his gums, something I did not like the look of but which I forgave because it set him apart from everyone else I knew, with their flawless identical orthodontics. In the zero-sum logic of my obsessive desire, any difference from them made him more mine.

Being alone all the time had made me secretive; it had also made me clever. Surreptitiously, I found out things about him. I found out what classes he took, where he had lived, that his father had been in the navy; when he arrived at school each morning, when he left. He was a swimmer, was training, someone said, for the Olympic team. This was at a time before the word swimmer was something people I knew used to convey a body type, and the information gave me hope because, after all, wasn't swimming solitary, did it not mean that he wanted to be alone? This I understood. Perhaps, I fantasized, beneath the normalcy that had fooled everyone else, he understood isolation. Infatuation has no reason, just frenzied rationalizations—anything to make the one you've decided to love more recognizable, more apprehensible to you. So I learned these things; became sneaky, learned to ferret out information about him from people I knew who knew him, without, I thought, letting them see how obsessed I was.

But what made me notice him first, when I was fourteen, what caused me to be obsessed, was none of these things, but rather a plain physical fact: his strange hair, not so much blond as colorless, the real blond burnt off of it from constant exposure to chlorine. It marked him indelibly as something different—not just different from the other people I knew but from *me*. His grin, his swimming, his blondness marked him as different, a stranger to my seriousness, my stillness, my darkness. Steeped in shame for desires I knew I mustn't feel, I assumed I was bad; how then could he not be good, more worthy of loving?

This is how your life happens: somebody has the right color hair. That year, in the English class where we read *A Separate Peace* and *The Red Badge of Courage* and in which we had to memorize Antigone's speech about divine and human justice, I would sit there watching him as he sat three desks away talking easily to the others, sit there taut with desire, speechless with wanting, learning to identify desire with impossibility.

In my desire for men there is always repetition, the hunger for a return to something I first saw and wanted, which was itself a reminder of something earlier; this is how it is with boys who want other boys, the mirror placed before the other mirror, the infinite passage of sameness reproduced so many times that it creates the illusion of multiplicity and choice and, finally, of difference. With women, though, there is only difference, true difference, and because of that, they can teach you something new. There was the middle-aged spinster in my Long Island high school, the one with the Boston accent, trying to signal to me from behind her thick lenses as she watched me watching the boy I loved, while I pretended not to see her seeing me but understood, from the fact that she was watching me, that I was in love. There was the slim catlike Homerist at my college who whispered cigarette smoke along with her corrections of our translations, who, because I could not seduce her, charm her into liking me as I would instinctively do with my male teachers, forced me to work for her approval, and therefore to learn, to be charmed by *her*. There was my graduate school mentor, an authority on tragedy, on women in tragedy, actually, who was so emphatically herself, with her cigarette-roughened voice and her elaborate artisanal jewels (which she referred to as either "pieces" or, more often, her "objects") and with the thin brown cigarettes she barely smoked because she was busy thinking about something, and you would sit there forced by the length of the still intact ash into a submissive anxiety; with the way she would seem not to listen to you as you feebly suggested something during one of your meetings and, two days later, return your idea to you, like a watch that had been fixed, infinitely more subtle and complex and mature than what you had thought up yourself—she was so emphatically herself that she forced you, by the very fact of herself, her presence, her jewels and cigarettes and intellect, to react, to be yourself, to think.

This scholar, this woman, who directed my dissertation, my thesis, which was, as I have said, at least in part about "brides of death," about the beautiful, young dead, the one I wrote (I now believe) because I had so early learned to identify beautiful youth with annihilation, recently showed me a long list she had compiled while writing an article about the Greeks' ideas about Eros, about desire. The catalogue is a list of images of disaster: illness, death, aches, chills, flames, suffering in the mind and the body, plagues literal and figurative, weapons, conflagrations, arrows, poisons, floods, battles, de-feats. These are the images that the pagan Greeks conjured when they thought about Eros. In the Hellenic imagination of the high classical period, love is always an affliction.

There is no gay man of my generation whose first experience of desire was not a kind of affliction, that did not teach us to associate longing with shame. No matter how long ago, how many times superseded by other, more successful loves, that primal experience brands us.

When you are hopelessly in love—I don't mean this in the sense of the cliché, figuratively, to suggest that my love was all-consuming, that I could not fight it, but rather literally, because from the moment I laid eyes on P. I knew *there was no hope,* that wherever my desire carried me it would never bear me along towards anything resembling completion, or happiness—when you are hopelessly in love, you may still strategize, still think of ways to weave your beloved into the fabric of your life, and thus to make him, if not "yours," then at least not wholly "theirs"—other people's, normal people's, happy people's. I strategized.

The first thing I did, in my mind, was to devise ways to think of him as being more like me. I would invite him over and he would look at my books and paint sets with bored politeness, since reading and painting were not things that interested him; he liked to swim, to play tennis. I started including him in my circle of friends, and at the parties they would have he would be the tiniest bit ill at ease, uncomfort-able but unfailingly polite. I hated him for his politeness, wanted him to give me an excuse to be angry, to have an emotion towards him of which I would not have to be ashamed. He would always be the first to leave. Despite my efforts, he remained, maddeningly, always himself.

When I saw that I had failed, I did everything I could to become more like him. I started taking the classes he took—science classes too advanced for me, classes that I nearly failed, much to the dismay of the mathematician. I started being nice to his friends, who had no idea what to make of me. I started swimming. It never occurred to me that one could love, or be loved, for difference.

This went on for several years, through the beginning of our senior year of high school; I insinuated myself into his life, knew his friends, his schedule, his parents, as though the possession of knowledge about all of his life could somehow reconstitute him, give him to me for my having. Once, during a sleepover at his house, I got drunk, and as we talked about the things that teenagers talk about at sleepovers, I knew that I wanted to do a kind of violence to him, wanted the intensity of my wanting him to break through, break down, the walls of his . . . his what? Of his *him-ness,* his self, his identity, what he inevitably and repeatedly was. But of course it did not. He was always himself, remote and somehow perfect, as if the fact of being wanted was a completion, an end unto itself; and I became more myself, over and over, wanting.

I think this would have gone on indefinitely, but then he began dating a girl I knew well. I watched them, in silence, and even if my eyes didn't go blind, my hearing didn't fail, the sweat didn't run from my body as I watched them, even if I did not go greener than grass, I was failing, becoming more locked within myself, less able to be in the world. He came to me one day and said that things were too intense now, that he couldn't ever see me again, that he could never speak to me again, and true to his word he didn't, and when he saw me in the halls or classrooms or cafeterias he would turn away, with an awkward- ness so transparent and crude it bordered on its opposite, ten- derness; and leave. I allowed myself to hate him, then, which was good, because whereas it had been forbidden to love him publicly, public hatred was perfectly acceptable. I derided his interests, his swimming, his friends, his hair, and entertained my friends, to whom by now I had returned, with biting accounts of my sojourn amongst the barbarians. This is when I first learned about sarcasm, and became, in those last few months of high school, the opposite of my former self, the shy and isolated boy who assumed that people who wanted to talk to him were going to make fun of him. As you might put on a mask, so I suddenly became someone quite different: someone outgoing, funny, sardonic. Despair and defeat made me popu- lar. *But all must be endured.* When you are a gay man you learn your irony early, since it is the thing that protects you from your own failure, the thing that allows you to look powerful, like a winner, when in fact you have lost everything.

—

The first man I ever had sex with had his name.

This would have been the week before my twenty-first birthday, in early spring of 1981. He was a year younger than I, a tall, handsome, and not particularly nice young man from a small Southern town. I have chosen the phrase "young man," a term that, for me, has no emotional or erotic resonance; had I loved him, even liked him, I would have called him a boy. He was cruel to me, and although he is dead now, I suppose I still feel a need to hurt him.

I met him at a garden party in the sodden Shenandoah springtime, a party that some friends of mine had brought me to, a party given by a group called the University Guides. The Guides, as we would call them, were a small and (as they would tell you themselves) very select group, notorious for the exclusiveness of their parties; for other things, too. The party was outside, in a tent. Pretty girls with blond pageboys, whose party manners—which they wore like clothes, like something you could take off when it was all over—did not manage to disguise the fact that they knew about, and liked, sex, were pretending to be shocked by things boys said. And the boys, these Virginia boys, who managed as always to be at once languid and fastidious, who unself-consciously wore their madras sports coats and paisley ties and, perhaps, kimonos—that year's fraternity fad, so outrageous that only straight boys could get away with wearing them—these boys slouched in careless *contrapposto,* swirling the ice in their third or fourth drinks, smoking, flirting with the blond girls with their hard, pretty faces or, less obviously but more excitingly, with each other. To me, who each semester would change my look—preppy, Euro, downtown, the way my grandfather segued through languages, as though what I wore would somehow help me to decide who I was—these dangerous and brightly colored people seemed to know something the rest of us hadn't yet figured out. It had always seemed appropriate to me that they were called Guides.

One of these young men was smoking in a corner, not flirting with anyone at the moment except perhaps himself; he just stood there, one hip slightly thrust out, a hand in one pocket, looking the crowd over. His glance lingered on me briefly, the way a fly might consider a half-eaten piece of fruit, then moved on. He had a smile that suggested he had a secret. I thought I knew the secret, and was so eager to show off this fact that I went over and asked for a cigarette, although I didn't smoke. He laughed as he tipped a pack of Merits at me; we chatted, stupidly, inconsequentially, since the unspoken conversation occupied us much more. It turned out he had the same name as my swimmer. Four hours later we were in his room, on a decrepit couch strewn with Indian blankets, naked.

I knew from the silly things he did that night—feeding me orange sections with his hands, at one point, not letting me wipe the sticky juice from my chin, which was oddly humiliating; other things—that he wanted to be thought of as someone who was decadent, and knowing this allowed me to forgive him, forgive him his cruelty in not talking about what was happening, pretending that this wasn't my first time. At some point in the night he said to me, "I've noticed you. Your cruising technique is *terrible*," and laughed. I tried to leave, but he wouldn't let me, pulled me back, knowing full well I was so hungry for sex, for even the pretense of connectedness, that I would come back to where he lay. When I finally climaxed I made myself say his name, closing my eyes as I did, so that I could at least have the experience of crying aloud that name during sex; but of course my consciousness of my own stratagems spoiled it. Later, he said aloud, half-asleep, "I've always wanted someone to cover my back," and curled up, waiting. Carefully, I turned my back to him.

Being with him was nothing like what I'd expected when, years earlier, I'd secretly dreamed of having a boyfriend. But it was the only thing I knew, so I stayed. He took me to parties with his friends, who frightened me not so much because of anything they did or said but merely because of their air—an air they clearly cultivated—of knowing things other people didn't know, of acting as though they were part of a secret that I still hadn't penetrated. "We were wondering when you'd finally show up," one of them, a medical student in an orange shirt, said to me as he handed me a rum-and-Coke, and the idea that people had known about me, were watching me, made me panicked and unhappy. How had they managed it, managed to know which drinks to drink, where to buy their clothes, which were not quite like the clothes that my room-mates and I wore? I sat there on the medical student's balcony and listened to them as they drank their rums and spoke their clever private language about things and people I didn't know, and felt like the butt of a joke. I had always thought that once I'd broken through, found the secret low door in the garden wall I'd read about, I'd be home, in a way; but this was clearly not the case. Each time he and I went out, I would soon want to go, miserable in the realization that even here, at the secret center, I was still somehow on the outside. But I had nowhere to go. By choosing to be here, I'd exiled myself from my old circle of acquaintances. So I stayed. Anyway, he had the right name.

But the wrong self. The last thing we did together was to go to the town's only gay bar. It was my first time in a gay bar; he enjoyed how afraid I was. Inside this bar, past a narrow counter, was a tiny space for dancing, but it looked bigger because the walls were covered with mirrors. A disco ball spun overhead. On the television, *Dynasty* was playing: a dark-haired woman with shoulder pads was screaming at another woman, a blond, also in shoulder pads. Everyone in the bar seemed to know each other, which terrified me, and at some point somebody put on a record and people began to dance on the wooden floor. As the handsome young man and I danced, we positioned ourselves opposite each other, but you couldn't really say that any of us were dancing *together*. Dressed in the same clothes, moving to the music that I would later learn to identify as typical of these places, a music in which distinguishing characteristics like melody or lyrics are subordinated to a monotonous, thumping, unchanging beat, we were avidly gazing in the mirrors, hungry to see what we looked like while we danced.

Think for a moment of Tiresias, the seer who warned Narcissus's mother and who, according to Ovid, had spent seven years as a woman before reverting to being a man. When asked by Zeus, the king of the gods, whether men or women enjoyed the act of intercourse more, Tiresias replied that women did; Hera, queen of the gods and Zeus's wife, was offended by the two males' bawdiness and struck the mortal blind. Unable to restore Tiresias's sight (since, as Ovid tells us, no god can undo the act of another), Zeus, in order to compensate Tiresias, gave him the gift of unerring prophecy—insight, if not sight. It was this gift that allowed Tiresias to see Narcissus's end, even before the boy was born, when his hugely pregnant mother stood before the old man in the glade and asked after her unborn son's happiness.

What is it like when two men have sex? In a way, it is like the experience of Tiresias; this is the real reason why gay men are uncanny, why the idea of gay men is disruptive and uncomfortable. All straight men who have engaged in the physical act of love know what it is like to penetrate a partner during intercourse, to be *inside* the other; all women who have had intercourse know what it is like to be penetrated, to have the other be inside oneself. But the gay man, in the very moment that he is either penetrating his partner or being penetrated by him, knows exactly what his partner is feeling and experiencing even as he himself has his own experience of exactly the opposite, the complementary act. Sex between men dissolves otherness into sameness, *men* into *de,* in a perfect suspension: there is nothing that either party doesn't know about the other. If the emotional aim of intercourse is a total *knowing* of the other, gay sex may be, in its way, perfect, because in it, a total knowledge of the other's experience is, finally, possible. But since the object of that knowledge is already wholly known to each of the parties, the act is also, in a way, redundant. Perhaps it is for this reason that so many of us keep seeking repetition, as if depth were impossible.

I have a friend who wrote a beautiful poem called "Football," about a young gay man who silently watches straight men play football, desiring them. The last stanza of this poem, in which my friend jealously imagines sex between the men he desires and the women those men want, ends with a description of a football-playing man, whom the gay poet-narrator secretly desires, "falling through her into his own passion." There was a period, in college, before the walking and hunting began, when I had sex with women, fairly often. This was never satisfying, but neither was it unpleasant; like participating in a sport for which you're the wrong physical type. You go through the motions in order to gain an understanding of why others might enjoy it, but it isn't really for you. From those indifferent couplings I do remember this: when men have sex with women, they fall into the woman. She is the thing that they desire, or sometimes fear, but in any event she is the end point, the place where they are *going.* She is the destination. It is gay men who, during sex, fall through their partners back into themselves, over and over again.

It is possible to fall in love with someone because he has the right hair, or name, or provenance; but not for long. The structure of the fantasy that your desire imposes on someone else is bound, in the end, to shatter, as that person's ("that man"'s) own identity eventually comes back to the surface, disrupting the image you want to see there. For most people, the difference of the beloved, the *themness,* is rich with possibility; for others, it is not. But for these others there are other pleasures, pleasures of a profound self-knowledge, the interior sight that is clearer than the sight of the eyes, the ability to catch the sound of statues speaking. I have had sex with many men. Most of them look a certain way. They are medium in height and tend to prettiness. They will probably have blue eyes. They seem, from the street, or across the room, a bit solemn. When I hold them, it is like falling through a reflection back into my desire, into the thing that defines me, my self.

The first—the only—boy I ever dated for a significant length of time was, not surprisingly, from the South. I didn't fall in love with him until one day when he sent me some pictures of himself.

He didn't have the right name; his name was Sam. The pictures were taken in a wood behind his parents' house in Alabama—or maybe it was behind his old high school. This was in December of 1988, and he was a junior at the university where I was a graduate student. We'd met a month before. I had seen him around, had walked past the desks where he was studying, noticed and liked his thinness, his nervous impatient gestures, the stillness at the center. His nostrils were delicate, like snail shells; they trembled when he spoke, if you got that close. I asked him out. His dark hair, when I finally kissed him, was glossy and smelled sweet, like a child's.

Now it was a month later, and he had gone away for the Christmas vacation. I was living in his rooms on campus because they were closer to the library than my own room was, back in the graduate dorms, and I was about to take my comps, and was nervous about not studying enough. So for a few weeks I slept in his narrow twin bed without him, and felt, while I stayed there, the secretive, almost erotically intense feelings—of an obscure possession, of a deep and almost infantile belonging, and of the giddy power that comes from knowing that you are trusted—that you get from being alone in a room filled with the possessions that your new lover has not bothered to hide away.

To this room came one day a letter containing the handful of pictures that Sam had taken of himself in the place where he'd grown up. He had sent me these pictures, I realized, to remind me of him, that he was there. Rightly, he did not trust me. One of the pictures in particular moved me, and put the seal on my feelings for him. In it, he was standing in a dull corduroy coat, his hair rearranged by the winter wind into the bangs he must have had in childhood, his face stiff with the self-consciousness of someone waiting for a shutter to click. Sam would later turn into a very handsome young man, but in this picture his face hadn't yet assumed the crispness of cheekbone and jawline that it would later come to have. His cheeks still had some baby fat, perhaps, and his eyes were round, and their blue pure, like a child's. Something in me stirred. Leaving the others in the envelope, I stuffed this photograph into my pocket, and decided I was in love.

A few years later, while I was rearranging boxes of old correspondence in preparation for yet another move—while I was in graduate school I moved every September for six years, but now I'd finished my degree and was moving to New York, to West Twenty-fifth Street, where my new life would begin at the center of the world—I came across a picture of a boy I knew well. I didn't realize I still had his picture. In the picture he is a solemn boy standing in a clump of trees on a winter day that has left the shrubs cracked, colorless and leafless. He is wearing a brownish corduroy coat; his fine hair, indeterminate in color—it will get much darker, later—falls in haphazard bangs. His mouth is slightly open, as though he were about to say something. His eyes are clear and blue. Not quite looking at the camera, he stares just beyond it. It is one of those old snapshots that have the date printed on the border. This one said FEB 67, so I must have been six when it was taken

In the summer of 1984 I discovered that there was an all-gay beach at the distant end of the public beach that served the community where I grew up. I went there. As I would learn from subsequent trips to this beach, trips I would make alone, looking for something I could not exactly name—not just sex, not quite love—certain fashions, in sunglasses or bathing suits or body types, would wash over the clientele of this beach each year: everyone seemed, spontaneously, to know what specific thing to wear on his eyes or body. This year, when I was twenty-four, everyone was wearing sunglasses that had tiny patches of canvas or leather sewn between the edge of the lens and the ear piece: they made the people who wore them look like people in the twenties, like people wearing motoring goggles. I wondered how everyone knew to wear them.

One day that summer, early in the season, a beautiful dark-haired boy in red-and-white-striped Speedos kept watching me, swimming near me. The refrain of that summer's big song, by the Police, was "I'll be watching you," and you could hear it scratching out of people's boom boxes, its resonances sucked down into the sand, leaving only the thud of a bass. I was by this time an excellent swimmer, but although I could swim near him, and we could nod in stupid mutual acknowledgment of each other, I could not think how to start a conversation with this boy. Each time I'd return to the sand from a swim, I would position myself in such a way as to be able to watch him watching me; and of course he knew I was watching him watching me, and would smile, but he never did anything. I expected him to move first. After all, he had those sunglasses that everyone was wearing; I assumed he knew much more than I did.

After a while this mutual watching became a game so absorbing and complex in itself that the notion of actually making contact with him began to seem beside the point. It was only towards the end of the day, when I was returning to my towel from a final swim, that I decided I would talk to him. I ran to my towel, dried off, turned my head to find him; but he'd gone. Putting a hand to my eyes, I scanned the horizon for him, for the telltale red-and-white stripes that had led me to him every time, earlier. But he was lost. On one side, the sun was too strong and blinded me. On the other, there were many men, but the lengthening shadows of the dying day flattened them out, reducing them to their identical bathing suits and identical sunglasses. Unless you got very close, there was no way to tell them apart.

When you log on to America Online and go to the area called People Connection, and then proceed past what are called the Public Rooms—chat rooms created by America Online that are presumably of interest to its subscribers, rooms with names like Senior Citizen Chat, Ethnicity Chat, or even Gay and Lesbian—to the Member Rooms, which are rooms created by members for themselves, you cannot help being struck by how many of the names of these member rooms contain the characters M4M—"men for men." A random count of any ten of these rooms typically yields at least half that are M4M. The name of each room is followed by a figure—the limit set by AOL is twenty-three—which records the number of members in the room at that moment. Consequently, as you scroll down the list of Member Rooms, which is very long and which can be a fairly good measure of the consuming if fleeting interests of the on-line public in general (OJ VERDICT, TALK ABOUT DI, PINOYPINAY, the last for Filipino chat), the screen begins to look like a roll call:

constructionm4m	23
BarelyLegalM4M	23
NJ M4M NOW	23
chicagom4m	23
NJM4M	23
wilkesbarreM4M	6
AlbanyNYM4M	12
losangelesm4m	23
AtlantaM4M	23
Boston M4M	23
MiamiM4M	23
dcM4M	23
M4MHomeAlone	23
NYCM4MHotel	16
CentralNJM4M	11

The list goes on. For the M-oriented M of New York City there can be as many as four separate rooms on a given day— NYC M4M, M4M NYC, NYC M4M NOW, M4M

NYC NOW. Occasionally there will be a variation—BLKGUYZ4WHTGUYZ, for instance—but most of the People Connection chat rooms created by America Online's gay male members contain these three characters.

The connection that the M4M rooms in People Connection are trying to make, for the most part, is of course sexual; thanks to several high-profile news stories involving on-line hookups gone awry, this information is no longer shocking. But for the most part, the connections made by the thousands of men in the M4M rooms come off without violence, or even unpleasantness. They begin on-line, with a mutual exchange of vital statistics between a pair whose names have appealed to each other; there follows, perhaps, a quick phone call, just to make sure he's okay; someone gives an address; a knock on the door is followed by brief awkwardness, which is swiftly followed by efficient and, usually, pleasant enough sex. This kind of relief is called "getting off," a name that conveys well enough the impulse that underlies these people connections, an impulse to be rid of something, an urge, a quantity of semen. On more than one occasion, after getting off in this way, someone will say to me, half-jokingly, as he leaves my apartment, where he has spent his lunch hour, "Well, at least now I'll be able to concentrate when I get back to work," and as I shut the door behind him I realize I feel the same way. But, of course, soon enough the urge returns, and the search for a new partner begins again.

Gay men like sometimes to think of themselves as hybrids of masculinity and femininity, but this, of course, is nonsense: you need look no further than at some mundane but pervasive an aspect of gay culture as the prevalence of on-line hookups to realize that gay culture is the dream of masculinity, a dream of a world of repeated and infinitely repeatable ejaculations.

Marriage and women have made this dream, if not impossible, then impractical in straight life; but the dream is frankly and unashamedly acknowledged, and accounted for, in gay life. At a house party on Fire Island last summer, a very handsome man with a shaved skull and beautiful eyes, a man whose attractiveness I made a point of resisting because he seemed so satisfied with his life, was telling me about how close he was to his lover's family—especially to his lover's sister and her husband. At the dinner table, which was fastidiously and rather beautifully set, and where sex was the recurrent topic of conversation, he recalled how he had told the brother-in-law about his and his lover's sex life, about how many group scenes and threesomes they had done, about how much the threes and fours and more had done to spice up their sex life, and about how stunned and, he thought, jealous the brother-in-law had been when he had learned of the superior inventiveness and numerical combinations available to the gay men. The handsome man's blue eyes glittered with self-conscious wickedness as he told this story. "He couldn't believe how much he was missing," he said of his straight counterpart.

I know many very happy gay couples; happier than many straight couples I know. These happy gay couples, when their relationships work, tend to stay together a very long time, longer, I think, than most of the straight couples I know who date. These happy gay couples live together, often work together, take interesting and exciting vacations together. One gay couple I know presides over lavish annual holiday dinners—Easter, Thanksgiving, Christmas—to which the same guests, year after year, eagerly come, come for tables laden with good food, and talk of interesting and funny things. There are children there, the children of people who had been children at the same couple's dinners years ago. Another gay couple I know made a pact years ago: that neither would ever attend a social function that the other couldn't attend. I think they have been together for nearly thirty years. These gay men seem happy, and, in their different ways, are happy.

But all of the successful, happy gay couples I know, the ones who show an enviable depth of emotional commitment, have one thing in common, and that is that they look for, and find, sex outside their loving relationship. This is a fact of gay life. I do not think that this vitiates the quality of their commitment in any way whatsoever. It merely suggests what is obvious about gay men—and, therefore, of men in general, since gay culture is nothing if not a laboratory in which to see what masculinity does without the restraints imposed by women: that sex for men is, finally, separable from affect. Threesomes, leather, orgies, role-playing—*playing*: for gay men, sex can be separated from the self, from the subject. Distanced, objectified, it can become, finally, aesthetic.

The way in which the names of the M4M rooms blur past your eyes as a visual analogue for the thumping, insistent, repetitive music you hear in gay dance clubs, or for the way that the gay subcultures, more than any other, it seems, spawn "clones": the repetition, the ostensible surface sameness, flattens you out, blurs the distinguishing features that make you *you* and, in the end, reduces you to the essential characteristics—your maleness, your gayness, your availability, the things that are, after all, all you really need to get off—so that you can return to your work, or your boyfriend. The repetition is not the problem but the point of it all. It is its own pleasure, the pleasure that is separable from love. The endless stream of M4M rooms, with their unchanging trio of salient characters—M; 4; M—blurs in your vision, an inexhaustible anagram that always spells the same thing: the urgent, impersonal way that men desire.

A yellowed print of the photograph that is reproduced on an oval piece of porcelain on the tombstone of my dead great-aunt, that Jewish "bride of death," hangs above my desk, next to a rubbing of her tombstone. The rubbing, which is about four feet high and was done on a sheet of creamy, feathery paper from an art-supply store near the Intersection of Desire, could not, of course, take the image, so there is only a blank oval space, vacant and sightless, at the top of the paper, where the image in the yellowed picture was. The image itself is aloof, solipsistic, hermetic.

Next to this picture, above my desk, is another photograph that seemed resonant to me when I saw it. It is an advertisement for Giorgio Armani sunglasses, and features a young man so flawless that the first time I saw it I stopped flipping through the pages of the fat magazine I was looking at, the bottom right corner of the page taut in my right hand, and—literally—stared. Because he's wearing sunglasses, it's impossible to see what his eyes look like. This doesn't really bother me. You can't ever really see the eyes of ancient Greek statues either—you only get the hollow sightless holes that were once filled with bits of colored stone fashioned to resemble white and iris and pupil. Since I'm used to looking at classical Greek statues, the eyelessness of this model seems quite natural. To me, he seems complete. If anything, the lack of eyes completes the analogy that is already forming in my mind, a comparison between this boy, with his glossy tight curls and the smooth white forehead that descends in an unbroken line through to the bridge of his nose, and a statue I've looked at often, the *Hermes* of Praxiteles, a fourth-century B.C. sculptor. Praxiteles' Hermes, who looks to be about nineteen, lounges in extravagant *contrapposto;* most art historians believe that his missing right arm once dangled a bunch of marble grapes before the greedy outstretched hands of the infant Dionysus—god of wine and, in a way, the id—whom he's cradling in his left. The right arm of the Armani model is not missing. The slender and oddly feminine hand that is attached to it (the fingers are a shade too long and taper towards the tips) is gently and not at all unself-consciously pressing the sunglasses to the bridge of the perfect nose.

You can't see the eyes of many of the pictures you get sent in the AOL chat rooms, for instance, NYC M4M NOW. These pictures often show just a torso, or a body from the neck down, or sometimes just an erect penis. The incompleteness of these photographs is due partly to a desire for discretion: some of these people who send these pictures are well known, or at least well known to others in the surprisingly smallish circles that constitute gay society in big cities, and for most men, the potential embarrassment of being linked to an on-line picture of a body sprouting an erection isn't worth even great sex. What is interesting to me about the incompleteness of these photographs, which are little different in their way from the alluringly posed photographs you see of "escorts" in the back of gay magazines (the escorts are likely to turn out to be the barman or student who lives down the hall, in need of a little extra money) is that they don't really seem incomplete—they seem perfectly natural to me, as natural as the eyelessness of the Armani model. The faces seem beside the point here: it is the bodies that excite, the bodies that through assiduous training we can bring closer to an idealized image than we can with our faces and their recalcitrant idiosyncrasies of jaw and cheek and nostril.

Gazing at the eyeless Armani boy and thinking, suddenly, of the headless AOL pictures, I realize that the former, which seeks to excite sublimation ("Buy these, it's like having great sex"), is essentially as gay as the latter, those unambiguous advertisements for immediate sexual gratification ("Call me, and you will have great sex"). It's the sunglasses, I realize, the eyelessness of him. Without eyes, he cannot be a subject, even the subject of his own desiring gaze; he can only be the object of the desire of others. What I responded to in the photograph of the dead girl, the porcelain picture on the granite stone, was the same quality I have been drawn to in the boys in the ads, and indeed in boys in person, since this is the look we put on, like masks, when we go to bars or clubs: a self-absorption so complete that it requires nothing of you but that you look. It is the expression that allows you to be not yourself, the subject, the desirer, the incomplete one watching in silence, but the object— the perfect, wanted one. The photograph of the dead girl suggested to me, at an early age, the power of images to awaken a desire that can never be fulfilled.

I know a man, a handsome young man with an agile mind and a brilliant professional career, who has sex with a different stranger every night, if at all possible. He logs on to AOL or goes on a chat line and talks to the men in these places, and almost inevitably one of those men will make the trip to my friend's small apartment—my friend will not travel to other people's houses—and have very pleasurable sex with him. My friend is good at sex the way that good cooks are good at cooking; he considers what is before him and works wonders with it. He works slowly, and with a self-assurance so profound that it transcends vanity, to make you have a good time; he enjoys the thought that he is someone who can do that for you. When you leave his apartment, spent and vulnerable, he will most likely offer you his number, and he wants to see you take it, fold it in your pocket and make sure you've not lost it, because of course (unless you already have a lover, which many of the people on AOL and on the phone chat lines do)—of course you want to see this sweet and smart and handsome and skilled lover again. As you leave his apartment, he promises he will call you.

Of course he never does. I have met people, strangers at dinner parties or friends of friends, who have revealed, as conversations move in the direction of sex or boyfriends or loneliness, the subjects that long gay dinner parties inevitably touch on, that they've met my friend, have left his apartment with his phone number and have tried to see him again; but he never sees the same boy twice. They seem perplexed, since he seemed so nice, so eager to see them again, but they are perplexed because they do not know what I know, and my friend's other friends know, which is that what he lives for, what makes sex interesting and compelling to him, is the newness of each partner, the thrill he experiences once he knows he has made a seduction. I often think of these men leaving his apartment, hopeful, and when I think of this what I am seeing is the excited gleam in my friend's eyes, the glimmer of the sure knowledge that he *has* them, has them more surely than at the moment when he was on top of or behind or beside or inside them.

My friend never talks about all this, but of course many of us who know him know it's true because we talk to each other and because at least some of us have made the trip up to his small dark apartment. What we know, those of us who have managed to stop wanting to be wanted by him, is that when he is not on-line or on the phone with strangers drawing them to him, he is at stylish dinners or clubs downtown or openings at galleries with one or more of us, and he will spend a lot of time wondering, genuinely and with some heat, why he has no boyfriend. "I'm a catch," he once complained at a restaurant in SoHo. "Why can't I get a date?"

I want to condescend to my friend, partly in revenge for his not wanting to see me again—for of course I was one of those who went to his place—and partly because condescension would allow me to feel superior to him. But we have all done what he does: the thrill of the seduction, the absolute pleasure, brief of course but heady, of knowing *they want you,* and before I condescend to my friend, wax clinical about narcissism and object relations, I would have to make a count of the boys whom I myself have fled once I've had them: the gentle and hopeful Southern neighbor whose breath was sweet with Jack Daniel's when we finally kissed and whose calls I stopped returning the next day, and who wrote me an angry note that I pretended to find amusing but then shoved to the bottom of the trash can, as if it might physically hurt me; the tall and beautifully muscled copper-haired man from the gym who, over dinner, after I'd found him in the locker room, turned out to be surprisingly shy and wanted to talk about writers and writing, and I condescended to do so only because I wanted to make sure he'd come back to my apartment even though I knew, because he'd told me, that he didn't like impersonal one-night stands, and when I finally got him back to Twenty-fifth Street and started unbuttoning his shirt he pulled back but finally gave in, and two weeks later left his last unanswered phone message on my machine, as I sat there listening, too panicked to pick up the phone; or the others, the men you meet on-line, the men whose numbers you get in restaurants and bars, the men whose notice is so precious to you at the moment you perceive it that you do anything and tell them anything just to get them, to have them, and once you do you need to have another, someone else, someone different, and so you must kill off the earlier boy, the one you'd been desperate to have the previous night, you must make him disappear because if you see him again he will become a particular boy and not just Boy, not just the thing that keeps you out all night or up all night or on-line all night in the hopes that he, like so many others, will pass through your small apartment where desire is something about *you,* something you can control, something, finally, that has nothing to do with the other person who happens to be in the room.

I was in an M4M room recently. In it, I ended up talking to a cute-sounding boy—his picture, the one he sent attached to an e-mail, showed him to be small, dark-haired, intense-looking—and I invited him over. He came and was pretty, as advertised. We undressed, had sex. Afterwards, while stroking him—he had beautiful, honey-colored skin that gleamed as if it had been rubbed with oil—I saw the marks on his body, tiny dark spots here and there, which, because I was so avid to have him, I hadn't seen before. Of course I was afraid. Multiplicities have given us an age of infections. I cleared my throat.

"You poor thing," I said, adopting a tone that might mask my fear and rage. "What on earth are *those?*"

The pretty dark-haired boy laughed, shook his head rue-fully. "I know, isn't it embarrassing?" He fingered the tiny dark blemishes himself, grinned. "I'm way too old," he said to me, "to be getting over chicken pox."

Sometime during my junior year of high school, in the middle of a winter that later became famous for a terrible and beautiful ice storm that made movement impossible, hung brittle trees with cracked blue fire, caused several deaths, a winter when I was no longer able to sleep—not because the ice-bound branches of the big willow in back of the house clacked against my window at night, which they did, but because my dreams told me what I did not want to know when I was awake—during this frigid and paralyzed season I could think of nothing but swimming. Perversely, all that ice, that immobility, made me crave water, made me want to be immersed in it, move through it. And so at school, where it was becoming impossible for me to concentrate in class because the bar graphs in math kept turning into the stripes on a bathing suit, I decided to take swimming as my phys-ed elective; and I continued to do so, as it turned out, for the rest of my high school career. The pool was always silent. There was supposed to be someone, some teacher, watching the pool, but usually, on gym days, because it was winter, it was just me and a not bad-looking senior in a white-and-green racing suit; and although I tried, I couldn't *not* see how the green stripe caromed over the lump of his penis. We left each other alone, swam in our separate lanes.

So here, in the element that was, above all, P.'s element, I tried to become him by doing what he did. Here, in this abandoned pool, in the freezing winter, I learned to enjoy the strict new discipline of water, as though the regularity of the laps I swam could somehow contain the unruly desires that were leaving me sleepless and ill that year. I knew that I had come here wanting to partake of him, somehow, and wondered if what I found was what he'd found, too: the infantile pleasure of near nakedness; the way that the water muffles the world and gives you back yourself, becomes a place where there is just you and the sound of your own movement, of your arms hitting the water and legs kicking it, a sound as regular and soothing as breathing; the childlike satisfaction of *counting,* of measuring your repeated progress through something that you can see, but that is, finally, transparent.

I still swim, every day. There are many reasons I could give for my daily, almost compulsive swimming. The easiest, most obvious—the one I'm most likely to tell myself—is that I swim for exercise, to keep in shape; this is perhaps the least true. To some men I know who work out with weights in gyms, who play games or even swim on teams, I say I swim because it is solitary, and (of course one means these things to be significant) I am not a team person. To certain other people, who may know more of my history, I say I swim because P. swam, and that swimming connects me to him, so long after all other connections, real or imagined, have failed. To others it is always possible to joke that it's an easy way to see lots of semi-naked boys—not entirely a joke, of course. But beyond all this there is something deep and unconsciously familiar about the pleasure in swimming, and it sometimes scares me, takes my breath away, to think that it was by the purest accident that I rediscovered this—the accident of knowing P. The pleasures of swimming laps are the pleasures of *men* and *de.* The pleasure of swimming laps is the pleasure of doing something that looks like movement but in fact goes nowhere; it is the pleasure of knowing that the distances you travel, however great they may seem, can always be counted in small, safe units of constant, comforting repetition.

If you hold Catullus up to Sappho, an infinitely long corridor of reflections opens up. If you lose yourself in it, you can learn something about desire.

The Latin word that Catullus uses at the climax of the first stanza of his translation of Sappho's ode—the part where the poet-watcher tortures himself by watching some strange man sit across from his girlfriend, talking to and looking at her *again and again*—is, as it happens, *identidem*. One of the reasons this poem was so easy for me to memorize when I was twenty and couldn't stop looking at the pale-haired boy sitting opposite me was the lulling rhythm of the stanza's two last lines, *qui sedens adversus identidem te / spectat et audit,* "who, sitting opposite you, repeatedly / watches and hears you"; the rhythm bobs along *identidem te,* the words that mean "repeatedly you," buh-BUM-buh-BUM-buh, and in a way it hypnotizes you, because if you repeat those two words a few times the sense collapses and you merely hear *idem* over and over, as though the poet were re-creating for you the experience of losing yourself, of collapsing in on yourself, that you get from giving in to your desire. How do you know who you are? You are the one who sits there in class, day after day, trying to memorize an ancient poem of love and of watching, repeating to yourself *identidem-te, identidem-te,* and although you know it means "repeatedly-you, repeatedly-you," it begins to sound like "*identity-you, identity-you,*" and I suppose this is really why it slipped so easily into my mind, a lifetime of reflections ago, because that made a perfect kind of sense to me. You, him, you *watching* him, you making your watching of him into another kind of love, you *and* him, it all becomes a blur, a furious repetition, the same thing, again, *idem-idem, identidem*.

There is another way to know yourself, of course, and that is not by identification with the thing you love, by collapsing into the other, but by differentiating yourself from it. I think that Catullus is aware of this and wants to remind us of this, to highlight these two modes of likeness and difference, to foreground the mysteries of *men* and *de*. Why? Because in ordering the words out of which he creates his own version of Sappho, he puts the adverb *adversus*, "opposite," immediately next to *identidem*, so that one of the effects of this climactic line is to make you hear the words "opposite" and "same" one after the other: otherness, alterity, and sameness, identity, are exquisitely contraposed. But there is something else, another kind of contrapositioning, here. The word in Sappho's Greek lyric that occupies the same metrical position occupied by *identidem* in Catullus's translation (buh-BUM-buh-BUM) is *enantios*, which means "opposite"—that is, what *adversus* means. So for those who know Sappho as well as her translator, who know Greek as well as Latin, the translation creates an odd effect not just, as it were, *horizontally* or *spatially*—by juxtaposing these two antonyms—but also *vertically, temporally*, by creating a kind of palimpsest, in which *identidem*, the repetition that is the root of sameness and thus of identity, is superimposed precisely over the space once occupied by *enantios*, by difference, opposition.

How do you know who you are? You are the one who loves by superimposing sameness over difference. This is the etymology of your desire.

III. PATERNITIES

Euripides' *Ion* is a play about a boy with two fathers. During the course of the action, an orphaned youth, an acolyte in the Delphic temple of Apollo, meets his birth mother, finds a loving adoptive father, and discovers the true identity of his absent, invisible father—the god Apollo himself. Because of its emphasis on parents, it is of course a play about identity, about finding out who you are by determining who gave birth to you, sired you. This is appropriate for a play set in Delphi, the place the Greeks believed was the center of the world, *omphalos tou kosmou,* "the navel of the earth"; for Apollo's oracle at Delphi provided, famously, the riddling answers to those who came seeking self-knowledge. Oedipus's fate was prophesied here, in Delphi; it was on the road leading from Delphi to Thebes that Oedipus, who'd been abandoned as a child and believed his adoptive parents to be his birth parents, met his real father, a stranger to him, and unwittingly fulfilled the prophecy by killing the old man. Because the young hero of Euripides' *Ion* is the mythic founder of the race that bears his name—Ionians—it is also a play about the identity of the Athenians, who were of the Ionian tribe, and therefore of Athens herself, of not just one boy but of his city and its civilization.

The *Ion* is obsessed with genealogy. In the prologue we learn that Creusa, an Athenian princess, has been raped by Apollo. After giving birth secretly to a baby boy, she exposes the infant, placing it in a basket with some tokens of his royal lineage: the golden snakes that are the emblem of Athenian royalty, an olive shoot, a piece of a sampler that Creusa had been weaving with a design of Gorgon's heads. She returns home, thinking the child dead. Unknown to her, Apollo's brother Hermes has been instructed to fetch the basket and deposit it on the steps of Apollo's temple at Delphi. Here the baby boy is discovered by the Pythia herself, the ancient priestess of the oracular shrine, and reared in the service of the god who is, unbeknownst to him, his own father.

Here, years later, when the boy has grown to adolescence, Creusa comes, seeking knowledge from the oracle. For years she has been married to Xuthus, a foreign prince who had lent Athens crucial aid during a war that, according to the Delphic oracle, the city was destined to win as long as the king sacrificed his daughters; this he did. The war was won. Although not of Athenian birth, Xuthus is rewarded with the hand of Creusa, the only surviving daughter; the grateful king makes the foreigner his heir. But the marriage, strangely, produces no issue, and it is out of a yearning for children—a yearning so powerful that Euripides chose to describe it as *eros,* a word used of erotic desire—that, years later, Creusa and Xuthus go to Delphi, seeking an answer to the riddle of their childlessness.

. . .

A few years ago a woman I know took me out for a coffee and asked me to be the father of the child she was planning on having, and I said no. This was in 1993. I was in graduate school at the time, was mired in a dissertation that I secretly didn't think I could finish, had no money to speak of, and although my friend assured me that she didn't expect me to do any parenting, I knew—if for no other reason than vanity—that if she had a child by me I wouldn't be able to walk away from it, and I couldn't encompass the idea of being responsible for anyone other than myself; certainly not a child. Like many gay men, I've been conditioned to think of parenthood the way you think of Lotto jackpots or airplane crashes—you know they're real, but you figure they'll always happen to other people. All this went through my head before I said no. "Well," this woman said to me that day, not noticeably upset but not quite looking at me either, as she traced circles of spilled coffee on the checked tablecloth, "I just thought I'd ask." I made appreciative noises, and after a while we got up and said good-bye. I heard she had a baby about a year later.

About two years after that conversation took place a close friend, whom I will call Rose, and who is straight and single, announced to me that she was pregnant. Since it's obvious to everyone who knows Rose that she has a talent for nurture—she is one of those people who makes things grow, plots of herbs and pots of flowers and friendships—the news made me happy. I had always thought she'd make a great mother, and had told her so on several occasions. Now, she was asking me if I would help out—if I'd be a "masculine role model," not exactly a father but a man who would be present in the life of this child. An "uncle." Unlike that other, earlier request, this one sounded at once appealing and yet not too involving, and so I agreed. I watched her grow round and pregnant; talked about names; sneaked self-conscious looks at Dr. Spock and *What to Expect When You're Expecting*. But after the birth of Rose's son, Nicholas, something strange happened: I found myself very deeply involved with Nicholas, who is three now, and whose godfather I was made at his baptism, when he was three months old. It happened gradually, and caught me by surprise. What began as a kind of ironic pseudo-paternal role-playing turned into a major part of my life. It is because of Nicholas—a real "boy"—that I now divide my time between New York City and those other boys, and the suburb where Rose lives with Nicholas. Nicholas and Rose have been absorbed into my own large family, who treat him like a nephew and grandchild, and her—well, like a kind of in-law. The thing you learn from having a child in your life is, Forget your expectations. So much, at any rate, for "no."

On a June day just after I graduated from college, I followed a beautiful boy down Bleecker Street, in New York City, without knowing where I was going. This was in 1982. I was twenty-two and had had enough of romance. I wanted sex. Romance had been for college. Romance was the South. Romance was the secret smiles of certain young men I knew at my Southern university, who'd gone to prep schools in Memphis and Birmingham and Chattanooga, boys whose careless drawls and rumpled khakis and haphazardly knotted ties seemed like invitations to equally disorganized and indefinable pleasures that, like the boys' slender and unmuscled bodies, had always to remain under the surface of a legitimate,

if mussed, propriety. Romance was reading rather than fucking. Romance was, especially, reading German, which is after
all the language of adolescent yearning, a language of which I
read a great deal, with a languor that was as self-conscious as
most of my moods at that time, on sofas and on spring lawns,
during my last two years at college.

Greek and Latin, to which I had committed myself in my
first year at the university, were different. Greek and Latin
were, first of all, adult, authoritative; they conferred on you a
kind of intellectual authenticity and power among your friends
who did not see the connections you could see—did not, for
instance, know that Greek's *hyper* and Latin's *super* are really the
same word, as are (you would joke to them) *herpes* and *serpent.*
But the vowels and consonants of these languages had no taste;
the pleasures of these unspoken tongues were austere ones, the
languages pristine, immutable in their singsong paradigms
(*amo-amas-amat*), as frozen as the figures on the black-and-
white posters and postcards of classical statuary with which I
had once decorated my bedroom and now, ten years later, had
hung in my dorm room: those two statues whispering about
the third; Bernini's *Daphne and Apollo,* a terrified girl fleeing
contact with an avid male, sprouting leaves where there had
been fingers; Canova's Cupid and Psyche, *Desire* and *Soul,* trying to embrace, and failing.

But German, one of the many languages my now dead relatives could slide in and out of at crowded dinners, was alive in
my mouth, tasting of rye whiskey and smoked fish, smelling of
my grandfather's filter-tipped cigars; it was, to my ears, the
rough-edged sound of boys' voices in the morning, after sex; it
was the sound of yearning but also of *having.* In my last year of
college I took a course on fin-de-siècle German writing
because I thought it was decadent; I wanted to be decadent, to

forsake romance for sex. I wanted to be decadent because I'd
spent the suffocating Shenandoah summers between terms
reading Christopher Isherwood, a rumpled Waspy boy who'd
gone to Germany for sex, and had found it. So these things
became linked in my mind: sex, and the South, and German,
and reading.

Now I had graduated, and I found myself, one day while
doing some errands, walking behind two young men who
were talking with great animation. The one who held my
attention was slightly taller than I; blond, with a heavy cap of
yellow hair cut just above the shoulder, which for that time was
slightly too long to be fashionable and seemed a bit dangerous.
It swung back and forth as he walked. This boy was wearing
long British-style walking shorts, and his surprisingly broad
right hand chopped the air occasionally for emphasis, which
made his hair swing more noticeably. His friend was shorter,
darker, less interesting to me. The first boy, the blond, was saying, bitterly, "He's driving me *crazy*."

Chop. Swing.

"I go over to his house, but nothing happens. I know he
likes me, so what's the fucking *deal*?"

Chop. Swing.

"I mean, what am I supposed to do, sit around at home
between dates with him and just jerk *off*?"

Chop, chop, violent swing. He ran his hand through his
hair, giving it a little yank at the end. I wondered what it would
be like to pull it, too. The sidekick nodded sympathetically,
made soothing noises; you suspected there had been other
conversations like this. They walked on, lost me.

I looked around; but no one was listening, no one cared. I
thought of Christopher Isherwood, of Berlin. I thought of
how embarrassed some of us had been, in a German class in

our Southern university, a place that often seemed hungover from too many decades of pleasure, too many garden and lawn and croquet parties, to discuss the significance of the languid *Schwertlilien,* the "sword-lilies," that adorn a public park in a story by Hofmannsthal. I thought, I've arrived. I am in a place where you can walk down the street in broad daylight talking about the cute boys you want to have sex with—not to romance, but to have sex with, to play with—and this was not exceptional. I was in the kingdom of boys. A place where getting the sex you want is innocent, really—no more objectionable than play.

For a while, in the mid-1980s, there was a place in the East Village called Boy Bar—a name that, at least to me, seemed satisfyingly decadent and Isherwoodesque—and here is where you went to meet cute boys. Not men: boys. It didn't look like other gay bars you knew about at the time: aside from a pool table in the middle of the floor and a big stuffed fish on the wall, there was not a whole lot going on in terms of decoration. Boy Bar—and how much fun it was to say that name, a name that made you pout when you said it—Boy Bar self-consciously eschewed the disco-era clichés of gay nightlife and seemed, instead, intended to resurrect some half-forgotten memory of a boyhood probably few of us ever had, a boyhood of hanging out shooting pool and fishing with your dad. We wore appropriate clothes: rumpled khakis, button-down shirts, long shorts, Top-Siders. At the time, it seemed quite radical. With self-conscious nonchalance we'd use the word "queer" of each other—not in the politicized sense that is now common, but, if anything, as a way of invoking other, earlier bad boys; to use the word "queer" was, if anything, to announce your own class pretensions and your education, an education that encompassed reading the journals of upper-class men—

Christopher Isherwood and his kind, for instance—for whom "queer" was the only available term.

Like "queer," "boy" itself, embedded in the name of this bar and forever on the lips of its patrons, was used with tremendous self-consciousness—perhaps because the avid young men of whom it was so often used were so obviously anything but "boys," and because it was uttered so preciously, with such a freight of desire and expectation, that it tended to put everyone of whom it was used in faint quotation marks, as if the ideal it referred to was somehow more present, more material, than the individual young man of whom it was being used. It was around this time that Madonna was making the term "boy toy" famous, and although she was talking about girls, of course—toys for boys—to my ears the rhyme suggested a metonymy: boys *were* toys, things you played with, and indeed the word often made you think of a thing rather than a person. Looking back, I am not surprised that Boy Bar was a place where a thirty-three-year-old man, like the man I'd taken up with during that summer of 1984, a person with high political and social ambitions that he would indeed eventually realize (the last time we spoke, he mentioned "the Senator" more than was strictly necessary), could keep using the word "boy" to describe the other young men he wanted, and when he did so you could practically hear the quotation marks around the word, the objectifying and aestheticizing force of his desire working on other men, turning them into characters in a willful private narrative in which he was the erotic hero, condescended to them, contrived to seduce them, and finally *had* them.

And why not? As long as desire is the force that shapes your interactions with other men, "boy" seems an appropriate way to refer to them. A boy is an object, something you play with; a man is a subject. I had been taught, anyway, when I was younger, that men don't play. They make.

What do men make?

On the first Friday of every month, a small group of friends—me and about three or four others—meet for lunch at a restaurant a half-block from where my former boyfriend and his current lover live. This is in 1996. The men I meet there each month are all straight, and in their late twenties or early thirties. They all write for magazines that are more hip than the ones I aspire to contribute to, and I find myself ascribing to them a knowingness that I like to feel I lack. These young men are bright and good-looking and have the easy confidence and self-conscious pleasure in their day-to-day lives of people who know they are at the center of things. Of course I cannot help asking myself how much of their ease, something I must fake, comes of being straight, and indeed my genuine pleasure in their company is always mixed with an anthropological curiosity: How do straight men live? It is interesting that I never think of them as boys, the way I'd think of them if they were gay men of the same age and education and class. Until recently I wondered why this was. I asked myself what was the difference between these men and the other, even older, men in my neighborhood for whom it seemed perfectly natural to use the word boy; asked myself why even a boyish straight man seems to have some core of masculine authenticity that evades even the most well-muscled, work-booted gay men I know.

One day, they're discussing an editor we know, a man approaching forty who's about to have his first child. The youngest of us, whom I won't pretend not to find cute and who is the closest thing there to being a "boy" in the Chelsea sense, grins. Dimples crease the corner of his mouth, and for the first time I find myself wondering what it would be like to fuck him—wondering not avidly, really, but not wholly disinterestedly either, the way you might wonder what your dinner companion's dessert tastes like. There is no question that he is the puppy of the group, and all of us, not only me, treat him with a mixture of faint indulgence and mild envy: indulgence for what he doesn't yet know and envy for what he has figured out, young as he is; envy, too, for his extreme youth, for the opportunities that clearly still lie ahead for him and are in the past even for us, for the fact that he is clever enough to know all this and forgive us for it. He is big and well built, but I always expect his sleeves to be too short, his wrists to be exposed, as though he were still half-grown.

"Whenever J. talks about this baby thing," this boy is saying on the day I find out our almost-forty friend is to be a father, "he gets as giddy as a schoolgirl." This remark startles me. "Giddy" is not on the list of adjectives you expect to hear used of a grown man with a career and a lover and a child on the way, and it makes me think about what I think I know about men and boys. I look at J., who is far from being my usual type and yet suddenly exerts a powerful fascination—an attraction based, I realize, on his very ordinariness, the unemphaticness of him. He is of medium build, nice looking without being as sleek as my younger friends here. His teeth are stained with tobacco, sexily I think (why sexily? because it suggests that he doesn't care what he looks like, that he smokes for pleasure rather than effect) and this, together with the tiny signs of approaching middle age—crow's feet, a gleam of gray—only enhances an underlying boyishness, just as the unexpected "giddy" draws attention to how centered and sober he really is, and this is the sexiest thing of all.

"Giddy," I realize, is startling because it gives J.'s sobriety texture, implicitly drawing even more attention to what is, I realize, the thing that seems to define him, the thing that makes him seem so obviously straight to me, which is his gravity, an essential and imperturbable sobriety. I realize that this is how I think about all straight men—they are *serious*. If they weren't, how could they win bread, bring home the bacon, provide roofs over our heads, except when soberly outfitted in suits or uniforms, dependable enough to be in the same place at the same time, day after day, mechanically, reliably, working, producing, making? By contrast, my gay friends and I are inhabitants of a culture in which libido is not subordinated to work but is, if anything, a product to be consumed. What are we if not the opposite, bent on adorning, enjoying, playing?

Indeed "giddy" sounds like a gay word to me, taunts me with the possibility of libido, and it is true that the word arouses me, as if hinting at some hidden side of J. that I might yet discover if only I excavate diligently enough, and so by the end of the meal I am doggedly smoking cigarettes in the courtyard of this restaurant with him, savoring a chance to be alone with him, not quite flirting but not *not* flirting, either. For the first time I think I begin to see why "straight acting" is a quality that has such allure in gay men's personals, and why the fantasy of seducing a straight man is such a pervasive and powerful one in gay culture (if erotica is any measure). It is the seriousness of straight men that invites the dream of seduction, tempts you with fantasies of perforating straight seriousness and locating and enjoying the libido—the possibility of giddiness—that is submerged, in real life, to work, which is what men must do.

Whatever its effect on me, "giddy" goes unremarked by the others. I wonder why. When I first heard "giddy as a schoolgirl," I instinctively braced myself for the wave of ridicule that, twenty years past the terrors of high school, I still expect to accompany any comparison of a male to a female. But they greet the remark with laughter that barely conceals with affectionate teasing a kind of envious wonder. I realize that whatever pejorative power "giddy as a schoolgirl" might have has clearly been outweighed by something much bigger here, and then I realize what it is. It is a very primitive and irrational thing. We can say what we want, but J. is fathering a baby. He is making something.

Children are the secret weapon of straight culture: they have the potential to rescue men from inconsequentiality. Fatherhood has the power to confer authenticity on men; it can be what saves them from eternally being boys themselves.

I was mistaken for Nicholas's father three times on the day he was born, and secretly enjoyed it. This was on a humid morning in August 1995. Rose had told me she was pregnant the previous December, and since then I'd found that I liked it when she asked my advice on a range of subjects: whether to have an amnio, where the baby would be born, what to name it. Rose, who is part Croatian and surprisingly sentimental for a mathematician, was eager to use family names. The girls' names she'd chosen were all rather pretty; some of the boys' names were quite odd. (Occasionally, when we were both punchy from hours of discussing names, Rose would jokingly threaten to name the baby after a great-uncle called Melchizedek. I'd roll my eyes and mutter something about how any kid called Melchizedek was bound to end up in therapy before he'd reached kindergarten age; we'd both giggle.) In fact, there wasn't much question about the name in case the baby was a boy, which I always knew it would be: Rose had always liked "Nicholas." I agreed with her that it was a strong name, with the proper Slavic pedigree. I liked it for another reason as well, which I didn't tell her at the time. Nicholas is the name of my former boyfriend's current lover, of whom I'm very fond, and who is very good-looking. Like many atheists, I have a deep compensatory superstitiousness, and I believe in the power of names.

We'd talked about names in May, while walking on a beach in Maryland that was known to me, but perhaps not to Rose or some other friends who were renting a house together for a long weekend, as a gay resort. A few months later, in August, on the day Nicholas was scheduled to be born by cesarean section, Rose and I woke at a quarter to five, then silently dressed and collected her things, with the exaggerated calm of people who are very nervous. Outside, it was still dark but already muggy, and I drove us the few blocks to the local hospital with the car windows wide open. At that early hour the main entrance is closed, and so you have to check in at the emergency entrance, which seemed a bad omen. The waiting room was totally dark, and we were the only people in it. A nurse came round and gave Rose a sheaf of forms to fill out; on her way back to her desk the nurse patted me on the shoulder and said, with practiced sympathy, "You look like a first-timer." She walked away before I could reply, and anyway, she was right, in a way. Finally someone took us to a room that had been prepared for Rose. As she changed into her paper-thin hospital gown, I caught a glimpse of her belly, big as a basketball and luminous as a moon above a thin secret crescent of dark hair. Quickly I turned my head away.

An hour or so later I was standing outside an operating room with Rose's sister Anne, a primatologist who lives in Puerto Rico and who, since Nicholas's birth, has enjoyed sending Rose an occasional photo of herself cradling an infant chimp in her arms. Anne, who looks remarkably like Rose—both have their Irish mother's old-fashioned, somewhat Betty Boopish prettiness, with big round eyes and small pointed chins—has a hilarious frizzy abundance of honey-colored hair, which somehow justifies to me my characterization of her as the screwball-comedy version of her more circumspect sister. I paced back and forth, and Anne asked me if I'd had anything to eat. "No," I said, somewhat smugly, feeling that this was the right answer. She clicked her tongue in the matter-of-fact way that people trained in medicine have. "Mm, not a good idea to go into a surgery on an empty stomach. You may faint." Almost immediately, I felt lightheaded. All I could think of was how, if I did faint, I would be caught out, revealed as weak, inadequate, unmanly. Just then someone walked by and said, casually, "You're not allowed out here unless you're immediate family." Anne and I looked at each other. "Well, I'm the sister," she said. Before I had time to think of how to lie, the nurse looked at me and gave me a broad, fake, bureaucratic smile. "And *you* must be the dad," she said, and walked away. No one bothered us again.

After a long wait there was a sudden flurry of activity behind the milk-glass windows of the operating room. Anne and I peered inside. Everyone was swathed in white and green outfits, grouped around what looked to us like an empty space: the whole thing seemed to me, for one insane second, like an avant-garde theater piece. The obstetrician, an angular, unsmiling woman who'd once been a midwife, was making a number of small rapid gestures, like a headwaiter at a restaurant table, above Rose's abdomen. Suddenly we could hear a baby shrieking. Anne and I started jumping up and down and saying, "Yay!" The door swung open, and someone pulled us in. Rose, who'd had to have a general when the epidural didn't take, was lying on the operating table, totally inert; all of the activity in the room at this point had shifted to the baby, who was lying in the corner of the room on top of something that looked as though it belonged in a cafeteria—a stainless-steel tray with heat lamps suspended over it. Somebody who'd taken up a position in front of this chafing-dish thing was reciting, very loudly, a series of numbers. From where I was standing, at the baby's feet, his nostrils looked like tiny valentines. "You must be the father," a nurse said to me. I started to correct her, but she hurried past saying, "Congratulations, it's a boy!" And so I just said, "Thanks."

Since I grew up gay, I'm used to imposture, to sculpting false identities for myself, when necessary, out of the silences that are other people's assumptions. The paradox of that day was that in allowing myself to be thought the dad—to be thought straight, that is, a mistake so easy and natural under those circumstances that it felt more like truth than the truth— I was being as gay as I'd ever been. The familiar thrill of disguise helped me into feeling what I imagined to be the thrill of fatherhood.

About nine inches of umbilical cord was sticking out of the baby's abdomen: red, pink, a deep, surprisingly nonorganic blue. The nurse handed me a pair of shears and asked me if I wanted to cut it. Holding the wriggling baby very firmly, the way an expert sportsman might hold a prize fish, she pointed to the right spot, about an inch above the navel. It was exactly like cutting the neck of a chicken; the flesh yielded with a slight ripping crunch. I stood there with the scissors in my hand, and everyone made happy noises.

Finally someone took the shears and put the baby in a trolley, and Anne and I were allowed to leave the room and accompany him to the nursery. They were still doing things to Rose. Like me, Rose enjoys Italian opera, and I think it was only half-jokingly that she made me promise, before she was wheeled off to the operating room, to track the baby, once it was born, from the operating room to wherever it was that they put an ID bracelet on him, so that he wouldn't get switched with someone else's baby—a gypsy's, presumably. As it turned out, there was no way you could have mistaken him for anyone else's child—he looked, and still looks, exactly like his mother—but as we rolled him down the hallway to the nursery, I nonetheless grasped the tubular metal rails of the little trolley they'd placed him in. At some point someone had put a yellow woolen hat on his head; sitting atop his wizened face, it gave him a jaunty air. He looked like Yoda on a bender. His torso was naked, and there still clung to it bits of the cheesy white substance that had covered him at birth, and which had made me relieved that no one had asked me to hold him just then. A blue clamp that looked like the hair clips my sister wore in our Long Island high school was attached to the remains of his umbilical cord, like a ribbon at the end of a pigtail.

It had been about thirty minutes since this child had been literally cut out of its mother's body, and a few minutes less since I had cut away the last traces of its anatomical connection to her, but already I could tell that everything would be different. I became aware of another thing about children: once they're in your world, they alter it, imperiously. They shift you in the order of things, displacing you, making you, in a way, incidental; the whole point of cutting them free—of uteruses and umbilical cords and everything else—is that they can leave you. When you're single, and childless, it's easy to get in the habit of thinking of yourself as the focus and end point of all your pleasures and experiences; everything's about *you.* Bizarrely, the only thing I could think of, as I walked alongside this baby, is that he would probably be at my funeral—that he would be when I was not. In order to be a parent, you must be able to countenance the fact of your own mortality. This stunned me, and frightened me; but it also, paradoxically, made me feel really connected to the world, part of the current of things. And, maybe, less of an impostor than I'd felt a little earlier, when people had thought I was his father.

It was thinking about my own funeral, then, that I bent over Nicholas as we walked down the hospital hallway. Suddenly he opened his eyes, which were a shiny, unseeing, intense blue, and seemed to look at me. "Hey!" I said. For the first time that day I grinned, and—a little stupidly, since what could he understand?—said it again. "Hey." Then I couldn't think of anything else to say, so I walked on silently, holding on.

After Creusa and Xuthus arrive in Delphi, Creusa meets the young acolyte who serves at Apollo's temple; although bitter towards the god who violated her, she is strangely taken with the youth who serves his shrine. Ion, too, is mysteriously drawn to this woman, and the two engage in a long conversation in which each reveals to the other a secret pain: for one of them, a missing mother, for the other, a missing son. The bond between the two is palpable, almost erotic. It is a perfect match.

Ion looks at this beautiful older woman and imagines that his own long-lost mother must have looked like her—this lovely, this aristocratic. "Your looks reveal your character," the teen-ager declares. "By looks, nobility of character is often to be judged."

Xuthus, meanwhile, has entered the shrine, where, in response to his entreaties to the god, he is told that the first boy he happens upon after leaving the temple will be his long-lost son. (Recalling a youthful dalliance during a visit to Delphi, the middle-aged Xuthus believes he has an illegitimate child living there. He does not mention this to his wife, who of course has had secret offspring of her own, which she does not tell him about.) As it happens, of course, it is the temple ser-vant Ion whom Xuthus chances upon after leaving the sanctu-ary; the older man falls upon the youth excitedly, embracing him. Scandalized, Ion draws back from what he believes are the stranger's improper advances, until Xuthus composes himself and explains himself. At first, Ion is disbelieving. "Your own son," he asks, incredulously, and knowing the ruses of the god he serves, "or just a gift?" "A gift *and* my own son!" Xuthus replies, joyously, unaware that he is Apollo's dupe. The two embrace as father and son.

And yet there is something not quite right about this sup-posed reunion. In the preceding scene, in which Ion and his mother feelingly discuss their mutual sorrows, the dialogue crackles with pent-up feeling and the sense of a submerged yet powerful connection between these two: you would feel they belonged together even if you didn't know they were mother and son. The "reunion" between father and son, in compari-son, feels contrived: you're told they belong together, but, like Ion, you have a hard time believing it. His real father, he senses, is absent, glamorous, mythic, distant; after so many years of dreaming what this moment might be like, it's inevitable that the flesh-and-blood man who stands before him, middle-aged, weary with wars and a private unhappiness, is something of a disappointment. And indeed, immediately after finding his supposed father, Ion is still possessed by thoughts of his mother. "My dear mother," he cries out, "shall I ever see *your* face as well?"

Until 1970 my father doggedly kept—and kept repairing—the 1957 Chevy Bel Air that was his first car. It was black and silver, and had fins. This car was always up on concrete blocks in our garage, bleeding a dark and satisfyingly shiny pool of oil that was to leave a permanent stain on the floor, which my mother tried for a long time to obliterate with jets of water from a hose, and if you ask me what visual memory I retain of my father in the 1960s I will tell you that I remember parts of his body—arms and legs sticking out from under this recalcitrant automobile—but no head, which is strange for me now since my father is a scientist, very cerebral, a great problem solver and dogged crossword puzzler, and as he has gotten older he seems to be becoming all head, the way babies do. (Like Rose, the mother of the child I have tied my life to, my father is a mathematician by training, and I am sure this has something to do with my connection to Rose—as if I, who have little sense of the practical, of the way things add up, instinctively attach myself to those who know how things work, how to make things.) Like a tangle of computer cords, the veins at my father's temples stand out from his flesh, pulsing with the data they carry to his brain.

As a child I hated the car, since my father's refusal to give up on it meant that we wouldn't have a new and more attractive one, like the ones that appeared every year on the driveway of our neighbor, who was (I knew from my parents' whispered conversations) a vice president of something. At the time, and a long while afterwards, I ascribed my father's persistence with this old Chevrolet to a miserliness that even then shamed me, my mother's child and the heir to her family's grandiosity and avidly curated sense of noblesse oblige, left over from a lost life in a dead empire; but I now see this is wrong. My father is, after all, someone who knows how numbers work, sees rigidly ordered connections between things in a discipline that, he insists to us, who do not believe him, is ultimately an aesthetic one; and I think his refusal to give up on things—his various cars, the Friday *New York Times* crossword puzzle, my mother, us—stems from a need to believe in the orderliness of things, as if any thing or person were merely the sum of its component parts, which, if you could only find the instructions, the theorem, you could identify, remove, fix, clean, and finally reassemble to create a better and more enduring whole. This is why I can still conjure the muffled sound of his voice, gruff with the effort of staving off inevitable failure, as he asks my older brother for some tool or another, and I can still see a grease-blotched arm, hairy and threatening to me, thrust out to receive it. A hierarchy of status and taste is already in place among us children, and I am never asked to hand him tools. Instead, I help my mother fold laundry as she watches Bette Davis movies, mouthing the dialogue to herself a moment before the characters utter it.

When my father drove this car, or any of his subsequent cars, it was his shoulder that would catch your attention, since

it was the only part of his body that moved. My father drives
with the severe concentration of the intolerant, as though the
grim force of his own intellect were keeping those other, less
alert, more foolish people from driving off the road and into
one another, or us. His face, while he drives, registers little
more than a screwed-up frown. But it is his right shoulder that
moves, every now and then, suddenly upwards, in a kind of
tortured shrug, as though he'd been trying to solve something
while driving, some crucial question about the direction that
his car or his life was taking, and had given up.

In the early 1970s, after the Bel Air is finally hauled off to
the town dump and replaced by a flimsy British car whose
interior panels start falling off soon after he buys it, my father
starts building colonial furniture from kits. These kits arrive by
United Parcel or APA in confusingly small boxes, and the
wood, when he carefully pulls it out of the boxes, smells clean.
In the garage, which is empty now except for the oil stain,
newspapers are spread on the floor where my father assembles
these kits, a process that inevitably culminates in the weaving
of straw seats, a process he clearly hates not because it is difficult—he enjoys difficulty, since it justifies his flinty brand of
stoicism—but because the instructions are inadequate and
leave him confused and angry. "There is no way that this piece
is supposed to reach *that* corner," he would snarl, tugging at a
piece of straw and glaring at the instructions, beads of perspi-
ration standing out from his smooth bald pate like condensa-
tion on a cold glass. As often as not he is wrong, and has merely
misread the instructions, but he will not admit this; as often as
not he ends up inventing his own weave, which I suspect
makes him happier anyway. Nearly all of the woven rush seats
on the chairs he has built have an oddly shaped, small but

noticeable hole in the center, the irreducible trapezoidal shape of my father's obstinacy, which you won't find on the store-bought versions.

The furniture phase culminates in the construction of a harpsichord in 1975, which, after months of laborious construction by my father, my mother, much to everyone's dismay, decides to paint blue. Blue is my mother's color. Her house is filled with blue things: blue glass, blue china, blue Delft ashtrays; huge blue glass vases are stacked in front of her spotless windows; she has lined the shelves on which she keeps her immaculate unused dishes with blue adhesive-backed plastic. Blue faience beads hang at her ears, the Museum Shop necklaces around her throat are as likely as not to have some bit of blue enamelwork. Whenever I return from trips abroad I am sure to bring her something blue, a piece of glass or ceramic that disappears into her passion. Her eyes are blue, as are mine, as were her father's.

So when my mother announces that she will paint the harpsichord blue—an absurd, a willfully wrong color for a musical instrument—no one argues. My father's province is construction; my mother's—and, by tacit and uncomprehending agreements on everyone's part, mine—is decoration. It is a paradigm I still find hard to discard. In anticipation of decorating the harpsichord's soundboard, I have spent a few months reading huge illustrated books about ancient instruments. When the time comes, I begin by tracing the outlines of delicate flowers on the soundboard in a wash of turpentine and raw umber. But at a certain point not long after I've begun to paint, my mother, who had studied art in high school and who had been an accomplished draftsman herself before marrying, decides that my flowers aren't vigorous enough, and adds her own impasto zinnias and dahlias to my weary blooms. (This is before she decides to paint the outside of the instrument blue; I think my weakness emboldens her, gives her the courage to demand more blue.) This curious hybrid of styles can still be seen on the harpsichord, which stands in my parents' living room, pristine and unplayed throughout the twenty years since my older brother, the pianist, went to college.

I think it is soon after the harpsichord is finished that my father turns his attention to barbecues, perhaps because they need no decoration. He will spend the next few summers designing and constructing a bizarre series of Rube Goldberg-esque funnels meant to hold lighted charcoal briquettes. "It's a simple law of physics," I remember him saying; the words make an impression on me, perhaps because the idea of physics, or of simple laws, terrifies me. "They'll burn hotter and faster if they're all bunched together. *Then* you spread them out." When my father makes pronouncements like this, about lighting barbecues or bundling newspapers or driving on expressways, it is with a tight self-satisfied flourish, as though each one were a point won in the silent and ongoing argument that is his life.

Some of the funnels my father makes are made from old cans of chlorine we'd accumulated when we had an above-ground pool. The pool no longer exists: we'd shared it with the neighbors whom my mother has stopped speaking to, and the pool is one of the more visible casualties of that rupture. My father makes vents in the sides of these drums with an old can opener, from the inside out, and the pointed peels of metal sticking out give them a sinister, weaponlike look. My mother, who fears chemicals and has regular conversations with the people at the poison control center, is convinced that the funnels will explode. But they don't. I think my father secretly relishes her fear; it fuels his eroded sense of authority. I can still see his face, eyes screwed up in concentration, as he watches the flames shoot out from the tops of the funnels, his eyes following the charcoal dust and burnt paint as they float upwards. The charcoal is, as he promised, very hot; the flames at the center are a pure liquid blue. My father stares into the fire. He is pleased with what he has made.

I met Nicholas's mother in September 1990, when I started temping part-time at the corporation where she works. Part of what she does involves complicated statistical evaluations, but I know that if I say this, if I say that she studied mathematics as an undergraduate and philosophy as a graduate student, you will have the wrong mental image of her: something Maggie Smith–y, maybe, all straight lines and tight, efficient features. But Rose tends, if anything, to an old-fashioned prettiness you associate with the 1920s. Her hair, which is generally dark except for one time when she returned from a vacation in Paris with expensive streaks bleached into it ("Do you really think it's all right?" she asked me in her high and worried-sounding voice), is bobbed, and she looks good in cloches. (My own mother has striking, strong-boned looks that remind you of her namesake, Marlene Dietrich; she has absolute assurance, at all times, about what to wear, and for the past five years or so has briskly dismissed all of my carefully worded suggestions about how she might want to wear her own beautifully graying hair.)

On her father's side, Rose is part Italian, and I like to tease her about what I think of as her Mamma Italia mode. There's always some glistening meat sauce, slick with pools of olive oil, gurgling on the back burner of her stove, which she won't let you sneak into until it's cooked all day. Since my mother was strict about what we ate, and liked a shipshape kitchen to boot, I love the easy abundance of the food in Rose's house, the overripe fruit stacked on a china platter on the kitchen table, the leftover chicken crammed next to Nicholas's blackening abandoned bananas in the ancient and cumbersome refrigerator, and in the oven something unexpected and totally satisfying, like a dill-and-ricotta pie. Rose, who talks to her butcher with the respect most people save for their doctors, will occasionally cock her head to one side after sampling some *soppressatta* or *pancetta* and, chewing with slow disapproval, wonder whether it's as good as what she got last week. In a way it was all this that first convinced me that she'd be a great mother, and that led me to urge her to have a baby in the first place.

Although she lost a lot of weight before she got pregnant, after Nicholas was born Rose got more hippy than she liked; her center of gravity seemed in those days to lie where the cesarean incision was made. She moved the way my grandmothers and great-aunts did, solidly but not without grace, swinging slightly from side to side. She is forty-four.

When Nicholas was about two months old, Rose brought him up to New York one weekend, and we ended up eating in a restaurant in the Village together. The baby slept in his carriage through most of lunch. When Rose and I were finishing up, he woke and started crying; instantly, two wet milk stains appeared on the front of her dress. After caring for a small child for a while, you develop an easy and unself-conscious familiarity with the functions and products of the human body: eating, spitting up, snot, peeing, shit. This I had counted on. Occasionally, when I was changing Nicholas, he would grin right into my eyes and pee quite gleefully all over me, the fine arc of clear clean urine aimed, it seemed, directly at my shirt, and I was relieved to find I didn't mind. Being made a mess of, which you weren't allowed to do in my house when I was growing up, seems to me now to be a proof of authenticity, that you are actually in the world, part of its unruliness and unpredictability. It occurred to me that my indifference to Nicholas's messiness was not without vanity: it was something I could wear as a badge of my own maturity.

But what I hadn't been prepared for was how being involved with Nicholas made me aware of Rose's body, too: her breasts, of course, which were a constant source of activity and attention around the house, but also, by implication, the places you can't see, the flesh out of which Nicholas was made and from which he emerged. It has been fifteen years since I've regularly had sex with women. Sometimes when I'm around Rose when she's nursing, or when Nicholas is enfolded within the curves of her body, I become powerfully aware of her physicality, of her as a woman with a body, which is not how I normally think of my women friends. Because I am a gay man, and prefer to think of the hard flat strong bodies of other gay men, which seem to me always to be a matter of protuberances and convexities, rather than the soft and mysterious bodies of women, with their secret concavities, it is not always an awareness I am comfortable with. I find myself trying to conquer my uneasiness by being clinical, by trying to think of how I might describe her body in writing. I can't help thinking, at moments like these, of how electrifying it must be for two people who are lovers to be the parents of a child. It had never occurred to me before that, more than being just the symbol of the parents' past intimacy with each other, a child is an ongoing vehicle for its parents' awareness of each other's bodies.

. . .

It was in the spring of my second year at college, in that course on fin-de-siècle German writing, that I first read Freud's *Leonardo da Vinci: A Psychosexual Study of an Infantile Reminiscence,* which is, among other things, an attempt to account for the origins of male homosexuality. Somewhere in his book about Leonardo, Freud writes, "In all our male homosexuals there was a very intensive erotic attachment to a feminine person, as a rule to the mother, which was manifest in the very first period of childhood and later entirely forgotten by the individual."

I should say that when I first read Freud's *Leonardo* I was less interested in the discussion of homosexuality, since I had not yet begun to think of myself as being homosexual, than I was in Freud's method, which was not as dry and difficult as I'd feared and expected, but if anything was agreeably familiar to me because it reminded me of archaeology, which had so absorbed me when I was a schoolboy and adolescent on Long Island, secretly seeking doubles of myself, eager to believe that unexceptional landscapes could conceal something remarkable and beautiful. Back then, as I pored over books by Flinders Petrie or Howard Carter's reports of the discovery of Tutankhamen's tomb, it never occurred to me that this process might be applied to a person—perhaps because the person to whom I was most attached at that point in my life was so dazzling on the outside that I could not conceive that she might have a richer or more complex or more interesting inside.

When I think about my mother it is true that I do not remember her body, which I cannot recall having ever seen: as stunning and as vain as anyone in her family, she last wore a bathing suit thirty years ago, before (she says) her legs got too heavy, or too varicose, or perhaps it was both. Instead, when I think of my mother, I think of her clothes. I have a few really great snapshots of her in beautiful, stylish clothes: in 1953, at somebody else's wedding and just before her own, she's wearing a turquoise taffeta off-the-shoulder party dress, smiling her dazzling picture smile and so entranced with the camera that she doesn't see my father, who looks surprisingly handsome to me in what was surely a rented white tie and tails; in 1963 she's standing on our front lawn wearing a plum angora sweater and purple Capri pants, holding a lighted cigarette and aping, I think, Lauren Bacall; her auburn hair is crisp and her lipstick is terrific and her teeth are very shiny. In 1970, en route to the fancy nighttime bar mitzvah reception for the son of a friend to whom she will soon no longer be speaking, she's wearing a turquoise velvet pantsuit and long, intricate silver Israeli earrings, the texture of whose filigree I would secretly savor when I clandestinely opened her pale-blue two-tiered jewelry case and sifted through the strata of pearls and chunky pastel-colored crystal earrings and the old charm bracelets, which made the satisfying sound of coins when you handled them; underneath there were plastic bags filled with the awful rhinestone costume jewelry her aunts and mother and mother-in-law had worn to her wedding, and which made me think, for a few terrifying months when I was eleven and I first found them tucked in there, that she was a criminal, had stolen these great gems, and that her life with us was a fraud, a front for a secret illicit existence of which I alone was aware. Now that I am a man, I am not entirely sure this isn't true. . . . In a picture that my youngest brother took in about 1982 for an art project, he has draped odd bits of rich fabrics around her, a black lace veil over her face, and a Persian lamb hat atop her head. Despite the Beatonesque absurdities of this costume, to me she looks completely natural, like the deposed empress of some lost civilization.

Nicholas's baptism took place in Rose's family church, in Greenwich Village, at ten o'clock on a cold November morning. A month earlier I'd bought him a beautiful Edwardian christening dress, and my friends here in Chelsea made the inevitable comments about the advantages of having a gay godfather. But despite months of planning, everything went wildly, comically awry at the last minute: we were late getting out of Rose's hotel room; the baby, who had since birth been remarkably happy and unfussy, started shrieking uncontrollably as soon as we got him inside the church; the priest started the ceremony before we got to our places; Rose's contact lens popped out as we raced up the aisle; the whole thing lasted about ten minutes, and so we were fifty minutes early for the reception that Rose had planned at a nearby restaurant, and the owners really didn't want us there until eleven, so after the ceremony we all stood around in the vestibule of the church or on the steps outside, pretending not to care. I was used to giving parties where nothing goes wrong and the whole thing works like a charm, and in the face of all this mess I found myself irrationally panicked: the failure of decorum seemed somehow so heterosexual to me, so typical of straight life, with its unpredictable children and last-minute interruptions and changes of plan. I thought longingly of my immaculate apartment, and of my gay friends, with their impeccable Heywood-Wakefield furniture and precision haircuts and perfect outfits and flawless dinner parties. (As it turned out, the reception Rose organized went beautifully. There were about forty people in the little Provençal restaurant, we ate and drank a lot, the baby enjoyed himself immensely, and long after dessert no one wanted to leave. We'd arrived well before lunchtime, and a few of us were still drinking pear brandy at the bar as dusk was falling.)

That evening, as I was walking on Eighth Avenue, I cruised, and got cruised back by, a very cute boy; it was like changing back into your own soft clothes after a dazzling but exhausting costume party. We went back to his place on Fifteenth Street. When he took his shirt off, it became obvious that he was using makeup to cover the KS lesions at the base of his throat. There was something unexpectedly sweet in the way his eyes met mine, half-apologizing for this particular last-minute mess, half-defying me to run away from it. Messiness is everywhere. For reasons that had less to do with this particular boy than he could ever have guessed, I felt ashamed for wanting to flee. We played very safely.

Men are patient, they wait.

When I was very little my father and I waited a very long time. This would have been in 1964 or so. We were returning from Miami Beach, where my father's father, a tiny, wizened, silent man who spent most of his time either vacuuming or fishing, and who I suspect never found his emotions again after losing his first wife and many of his siblings in the Spanish flu epidemic of 1918, had had a heart attack. Until he died, much later, nobody knew that his given name was Abraham, like that of my other, more loved grandfather; everyone called my father's father Al, and we'd always assumed his real name was Albert. But then, he did not speak much about his life, or his past.

My father and I had flown down to see him, and even then, small as I was, I wondered why we bothered, since my father's parents seemed so remote, lacking the single-minded and smothering attentiveness that my mother's father gave his only child and which for me was the standard of all parental love. Now, thirty years later, I wonder about different things. I cannot imagine, for example, what my father said to his father, since both of them were so often so uncommunicative; perhaps my father talked instead to his mother, an anxious and clever woman who was terrific at all kinds of card games, at mah-jongg and at picking winning horses; who once each week towards the end of her long life would put on a mink stole and, accompanied by her three sisters—all of them rail-thin, all of them chain-smoking—take three buses to get to the race track where they would all bet on dog races; who painted her nails and never seemed quite sure about the names of her third son's children. I don't know. I do know that we went, and that when we flew back there was bad weather in New York and we circled for hours over Kennedy Airport. Uncomplainingly—for I was as silent with my father as he was with his—I counted the moon go past my window so many times that I fell asleep. My parents used to like to tell the story of my father's and my seemingly endless return home that night as a parable about my goodness, about how well behaved a child I had been; but to me, now that I have had some experience of what small children are like when they must wait, it seems a parable about my father and his patience, his goodness.

Ten years later, my father's father died in a hospital on Long Island to which my father and his older brother had brought him, and, during the weeks that this shrunken old man lay dying, my father would visit every day on his lunch hour. I can't imagine that they spoke much during those daily visits, but I do know that my father, who hated hospitals, went every day, eating his lunch, I suspect, in more or less complete silence as his own father lay oblivious to him on the high stiff bed, dreaming of his dead wife and dead brothers and sisters. This went on for several weeks. Since no one bothered to call my father at work the morning that his father finally did die, he went to the hospital as usual that day, ready to sit patiently at this strange and silent man's bedside, not saying much but merely being there. But the bed was empty, folded up. The brief time during which the significance of the vacant bed was sinking in, the three or four minutes before he had to go talk to someone about where to find his father's body and what needed to be done with it, were probably among the few in my father's life that he wasn't waiting for someone.

The bodies you see up and down the streets of Chelsea, on Eighth Avenue, parading at the Intersection of Desire, are the result of many hours of hard work, but it would be a mistake to say that they are all the same: there are swimmer's bodies, which are "defined" but not huge; gym bodies, which are big, but still reasonably proportionate; and body-builder bodies, which for all their extremeness always seem oddly unfinished, as though the clearly demarcated hunks of muscle were waiting to be made into something else—dog food, perhaps, or sausage. Looking at them, you can't help sensing the effort that went into them. There are other bodies, though, that you occasionally notice as well. These are the bodies of young men that have begun to fail. The skin on these bodies, which is the same wizened orange that my great-aunts in Miami Beach had, seems eager to part company from the flesh beneath; the skulls are already visible beneath the faces; the hair is lank and thin.

The limbs are, anomalously, covered. As different from each other as they are, though, both kinds of bodies seem more generic, somehow, than the kind of body you used to think of as being "normal": they have come to belong to the realm of the symbolic. When you see them, you're less apt to think of the people—or, rather, the personalities—that inhabit them than you are to think "gym" or "sex" or "AIDS." It's as if the extremes of strength or disease have squeezed out any space for the particularity of personality, or history. All that's left is bulk or wasting, excess or lack.

I have lived here so long that it seems odd that, when I think of a "normal" male body, I think of my father's body as I used to see it when I was a child: neither tall nor short; less attractive than functional; and, at least on weekends, often covered with a mixture of sweat and motor oil, or sweat and grass cuttings, sweat and sawdust, sweat and charcoal dust, or just sweat. It would never have occurred to me to describe it; it merely was. The well-muscled gay man's body today seems, by contrast, like something decorated, embellished. This is ironic because, in a way, this body seems clearly to be an attempt at recuperating masculinity, a visible sign of adequacy and power and legitimacy to be displayed proudly by those who, as children, may have been taunted for being too thin or too weak or too clumsy. Once, when I was about eleven, on a very hot summer day, I was ordered to help my father cut some shrubbery. I couldn't lift the electric hedge cutter; misinterpreting his laughter—or perhaps not—I was humiliated. I waited till he'd gone in to eat something, and then, with a pair of clippers, stood in the sun and hacked away until I fainted from dehydration. Not long after I secretly bought something advertised as a chest expander, and I worked with it at night, with the door shut carefully behind me.

Gay men's bodies are the bodies of men who do not want to feel shame before their fathers. But there is no way to get one of these bodies without assiduously working at it, which is of course something our fathers would never have done.

In his *Leonardo,* Freud writes, " . . . the boys whom the growing adult now loves are only substitutive persons or revivals of his own childish person, whom he loves in the same way as his mother loved him."

In the fall of 1992 I was in love for six weeks with a man who had perfected a peculiarly childish handwriting to go with his boyish looks. This man, whose whole professional life was devoted to style, as it happens—he got paid very well for arranging the rooms of houses to be photographed in upscale interior design magazines—sent me many notes during those six weeks, all printed in a surprisingly unkempt and scratchy schoolboy's writing, the naiveté of which, I now realize, was as carefully studied as his flower arrangements. ("The only way to do roses is to cut them *way* down," he told me on our first date, biting his lower lip adorably as he viciously sliced off the stems of some white flowers I'd brought.) His clothes were a grown man's version of the schoolboy clothes he would have worn had he indeed gone to prep school—had his rich and profligate grandfather not squandered the family money, as he often told me, eager to provide a rich and interesting narrative for himself, as though there weren't enough of him to be visible without one. I knew many young men in college who wore those clothes thoughtlessly; they'd never have ironed their khakis. In the many phone messages that he left on my answering machine during those weeks—he was living in New York, and I was still in New Jersey, where I was in graduate school reading about brides of death—he'd say "um" a lot, as though he were a shy and studious child of nine.

I am not unaware that as I write this I am trying to convey a certain detachment from Brad's meticulously realized boyishness, as though it weren't the core of what charmed me about him. But it was. It was the thing about him that I found irresistible, and if it was irresistible, it was not least because these certain details—the lower lip bitten in concentration, the scrawled notes, the "ums"—gave me access once again to my own lost and unhappy boyhood, as though by loving Brad I might be able to recuperate and repair something in me that hadn't been what it should, something damaged.

Sometimes when I walk around my neighborhood I think that this is not really a culture of desire but rather a culture of play—a culture of damaged boys seeking, like me, to recover and then reexperience, with more joy and fewer restraints, their own lost boyhoods. Desire and sex are just an expression of an almost willful insistence on constant play. Playfulness is what differentiates gay style from straight style, just as the sheer amount of play that is available, at least in theory, to my middle-class gay neighbors here in Chelsea differentiates gay men's lives from their straight counterparts' lives, which are derided for being dull. Here in Chelsea, the gay ideology of play means weekends on Fire Island, with their rigidly scheduled naps and cocktail hours and dinners and late-night slots for clubbing and sex; the party circuit and circuit parties; bars, dance clubs, and sex clubs; drag dinner parties; and endless sequences of drugs to make you dance or to make you feel sexier or more loving or merely to keep you awake while you play.

This hyperactivity sometimes strikes me as manic, as a way of putting something off—though it wasn't until I'd spent some time with children that I realized just what it is that the illusion of endless choice, of infinite possibilities for fun and limitless potential for activity, seeks to delay indefinitely. Sometimes, on the other hand, the culture of playfulness makes total sense to me. Without anyone but yourself to be responsible for—to wait for—there is no reason, really, not to play.

The first thing other than Rose's body that Nicholas loved was the moon. I loved this about him; to me, it made him seem poetic, and more textured than I'd ever suspected anyone under thirty could be. When he saw the moon in a picture book, like the very famous and beautiful one called *Goodnight Moon* ("Goodnight, air" goes my favorite of its lulling final pages), he'd exclaim, "A-moo!" and look up to me excitedly for confirmation while stabbing the book with a stubby forefinger. I'd nod and say, "Yes, that's the moon." It was a mystery to me how he came to recognize the moon in its various phases, both in books and, now that he is older, in the sky; I wondered how he knew that both the circles and the crescents to which he'd so furiously point were the same object. Some nights he'd make me take him to each window in Rose's house before going to bed, hunting for the moon, and his face would get very serious and he'd do his looking-bashfully-out-from-under-the-brows thing, peering anxiously at the night sky. When it was there, he'd point wildly and say "A-moo!" Occasionally, when he woke up crying in the night, I'd go to his room and stand in front of his crib, rubbing his back and saying, "Do you want to see the moon?" and sometimes he'd already be asleep again by the time I got him out of the crib and into my arms and over to the window. I think he was comforted just by the sound of the word *moon,* which, I learned again, is as soothing as the thing itself.

It's a cliché of love between adults that it makes the world seem new, but that is not true. What's new is the lover: the things you are supposedly seeing again as if they were new are in fact just instruments, not objects in themselves—so many lenses through which the novel image of your lover is constantly refracted. But everything in the world really *is* new to a baby, and because you have to explain everything to a child, it all becomes new to you, too. Babies force you to confront the most basic things—things you're likely to have taken more or less for granted for most of your adult life, things like the moon or a door—and make you really see them again. In so doing they also make you into authors; things only live and become real in your descriptions of them. This is a baby's gift to you. Even when I am at home, alone at night, in my apartment in New York, I find myself looking out the window, scanning the sky for the moon's newly familiar face.

Since he was about three months old, Nicholas has been a beautiful child. Until then he had the same rumpled and paradoxically old-looking face that many infants have, but when he turned three months, I became struck by his beauty. His head is large and round, except for a funny bump at the very back, which I always feel for when I am cutting his hair, something I will not let anyone else do; his forehead is high and clear; his eyes, which even strangers on the street stop us to look at, are startlingly, almost unnaturally large, wide-spaced, and blue. Because of their color, there was a time when some of my friends thought that Nicholas must really be my own son—I mean my biological son. But my eyes are nothing like his, which are a deep, opaque blue, like enamel. His face, underneath fine cornsilk of a still indeterminate color—light brown?

dark blond?—ends in a pointed chin, like his mother's. He will, I think, be tall, unlike me.

To my mother I think it was very important that her children be beautiful—although not, to be fair, for superficial reasons of vanity. Being beautiful, along with dying young, was a crucial part of her family's sense of who they were, of their special place in a history in which beauty and tragedy were inseparable. To be beautiful in my mother's family was a proof of legitimacy. It's odd how often it turned out, in the many stories I eagerly heard as a child from her father, that man of many and sometimes cruel vanities who fastidiously coordinated the colors of his various outfits each morning, that the failures in the family, the ones who married badly or had poor manners and business reversals, were ugly. *By looks,* Ion says, *nobility is often to be judged*; and for my grandfather, too, moral failure and aesthetic shortcomings were indistinguishable. *Kein' feinkeit*—"No refinement"—he would say now and then, dismissively, of some brother or cousin, and you could never be sure whether he was referring to their messy lives or to the fact that his family's deep-set eyes and strong jawline had somehow, by an unfair accident of genetics, bypassed them.

When I first moved to New York, I found myself living in a culture in which the line between looks and character had also become blurred—though this time by desire rather than vanity. Who you were in the scheme of things was a function of how you looked. Since I'd been prepared for it all my life, I didn't find this at all strange. What is important in Chelsea, moreover, is the same thing that was important for my mother's father: that everyone look the same, that they fit an undefined but readily identifiable template of beauty.

When I was thirteen, immediately after my bar mitzvah, I started investigating my family history, and have come to know the faces of the dead much better than I know the faces of the people who live in my apartment building. Since I am the keeper of many family photographs, some of them over a hundred years old by now, I know what these relatives looked like, and can see the traces of their faces in those of my parents and cousins and siblings. One of my younger brothers is a double for our great-uncle, a brother of my father's father, a jazz musician who was one of those who died in 1918 of Spanish flu, at twenty. He collapsed after driving three hundred miles on a motorcycle through a snowstorm to see his fiancée, who'd been taken ill; she survived, and sixty years later, when she was another man's widow, she still spoke of this dead boy, her eyes wet with desire more than grief. My sister, who is a journalist, has something about her of my father's aunt, a wiry woman with a comical rubbery nose, whose fifteen-year-long correspondence with me about family history suggests to me, at least, that she herself could have been a professional writer. Her lack of sentiment appalled me, and clearly identified her as part of my father's family, who lacked the rich and elaborately self-justifying narratives with which my mother's relatives adorned themselves, as though the stories were as crucial as clothes or makeup.

And indeed my father's side of the family had no great claims to beauty; it was my mother who, looking through her in-laws' ancient crumbly photograph albums, would invent beauty for them, crying aloud, "But look, look how *beautiful* she was!" My father's family just lived, and when they died young, as many of them did, they got no legends in return, but merely slid into anonymity. All of my paternal grandfather's nine siblings died before they were twenty, and no one even knew their names until I went down to the Municipal Archives and spent two weeks in the summer of 1995 tracking them down. It never occurred to my father's father to tell us what they looked like.

Because, as I have said, I am the custodian of my family's stories and photographs, I also know exactly which are the faces that haunt my own: the set of my jaw and the shape of my face are the same as that of my mother's uncle, who together with his wife and four teenage daughters was executed by the Germans during the war—a fact, I cannot pretend not to know, that has only enhanced their collective beauty over the past half-century; something around my eyes used to remind my older relatives, while they lived, of that man's sister, the one who died in 1923 at twenty-six, *a week before the wedding*, as my grandfather would say. As a child I relished hearing the exclamations of old relatives, who would soon be dead, about which of their already dead sisters or brothers I looked like. These cries of recognition gave me my first clear sense of who I was, and who I was turned out to be a kind of puzzle, something you couldn't guess from my last name, my father's name, the name of all those people I didn't look like.

My mother, too, would tell me stories about her relatives when I was little; sometimes in my mind they would get confused with the plots of the old movies she would watch—*Now, Voyager* or *The Secret Garden*—pictures, as it happens, in which beauty was transformative, where looks were a plot point. "See how *beautiful* she was," she'd say again, but here she was referring to Bette Davis's triumphant metamorphosis from a withered spinster into a woman of the world. Sometimes I would agree that the dead relative's face was indeed beautiful; sometimes, when I didn't agree—as was the case with another aunt of hers, the woman who was forced to marry her dead sister's fiancé, who never struck me as being much more than generically pretty—I would assume that my own standards for beauty were defective, and I would say nothing. For the stories didn't make sense without the beauty: Why would her poor aunts have been forced to marry their ugly richer cousin, unless they had had something to offer that an ugly rich man would want—beauty? Why had a photograph of her impoverished fatherless mother—a photograph that now lies, embalmed in plastic, in a mahogany cabinet that Rose inherited from her aunt and subsequently gave to me—been chosen to adorn an ancient Lower East Side shop window, unless she had been beautiful? A great-aunt, writing to me in 1973 from Haifa in response to a letter in which I'd asked her for family informa-tion, described my mother's Uncle Sam, the one who did not, in the end, escape the Germans. "He had the wife Ester and four daughters," she wrote, and then went back and inserted the word *beautiful* between "four" and "daughters," the way you'd go back and correct an exam paper. In the stories of my mother's family, beauty is necessary, cleansing, justificatory: it generates the best and most vivid narratives, and redeems the worst imaginable suffering.

My homosexuality, when I first acknowledged it, stopped hiding from it, seemed less a surprise than a kind of fulfillment. It seemed appropriate that I now belonged to a world that existed in an eternal present, because it had no generations: the same world I had been inhabiting for years, in my hours among photo albums that were eczematous with age, shedding flakes of black paper every time I picked them up. In a picture, it is always Now. In a picture, if you're lucky, you are always beautiful.

The stories I know make no sense without those faces, just as I myself make no sense without the stories. One of the things I worry about when I think about my relationship with

Nicholas, which is sometimes paternal and sometimes not, is that the stories that I know so well, the ones I can tell him because I heard them from my grandfather, won't go with his face, which is so completely his own. Unconsciously, inevitably, we seek in lovers or even tricks the things that we need to confirm or recover, tics and traits that remind us of something; from Nicholas I have learned that this is not an option with children. They are irreducibly their own people, supreme in their own difference. The thing is, you can't break up with them.

In the fall of 1996 I started staying with Rose and Nicholas a few days every week. At the time I told myself that it was a matter of convenience, since I'd been asked to teach a course twice a week in the classics department at Princeton, just a few stops on the commuter line from the one you'd get off at to visit Rose and Nicholas, and it made more sense for me to stay with them than to keep taking the train back to New York after each class. So I would take the train down on a Monday evening or Tuesday morning, right before class, and stay through to the end of the week. Most of my life I have managed to be doing more than one thing at a time—jobs, plans, boyfriends, whatever—and I'd always thought that having a superabundance of possibilities meant that I was free. To my mind, being unfettered was the whole point of being gay: you moved to places like Chelsea in order to have limitless choice. Now, in the fall of Nicholas's second year, I'd gotten locked into a regular routine for the first time, and found I didn't mind as much as I'd expected. The long rocking commute between New York and where Rose lives gave my life a predictable rhythm that was, in its own way, liberating—it sounds funny to say, but it freed me from wondering what would happen to me all the time. I knew that each time I got off the train, Rose would be waiting at the station, and Nicholas would be in the car seat in back, saying, "Da!" which I knew doesn't mean "Daddy"—many people would get this wrong—but instead was his word for "Hello."

Still, the commuting also makes me feel fraudulent, sometimes. I occasionally wonder whether I like the commuting not because it makes my life more regular, but because it allows me to continue being in two places at once. Sometimes I board the train at Penn Station in New York, and as I take my seat I notice all the businessmen, some my own age, many much older, but all clearly an identifiable thing, members of a category you could name at a glance. I look at these men, who probably assume about me what I assume about them, and I think, No. Oh, no. I'm not one of you.

At around the time I started this regular commute, I let my gym membership lapse. I told myself that it was because I wasn't in New York often enough to justify it, but the truth was that I'd lost interest long before. In addition to my swimming, I'd worked out with weights pretty much like everyone else I knew; I was satisfied with the results. Then, when Nicholas was about four months old, I developed a bad case of swimmer's shoulder and was instructed not to swim for two months. During that time, when I was doing remedial weight lifting, the weight room at the YMCA where I went began to strike me as slightly absurd. The critic Henri Bergson defines comedy as the imposition of the mechanical on the organic, and it's true that once you abandon the basic premise of body culture—that you need a good body in order to live longer or, more crucially, to have better sex—once you discard the ideological context, the barbells and rowing machines and cycles and bench presses seem vaguely hilarious, like the machine that, with solemn regularity, inserts food into Charlie Chaplin's mouth in *Modern Times*. I would think of my father, dusty and stained in the garage as he hammered and sawed and brushed, making things. So I quit.

There is no getting away from the fact that since then, my body has changed. I've lost the padding of muscle on the caps of my shoulders; the muscles running down the sides of my torso, which on every swimmer get quite big, are eroded; and for the first time in my life my stomach isn't quite flat. In my neighborhood people only talk about their bodies getting bigger, or at least their plans to increase the size of their bodies; you forget that they can regress as well. I hadn't really noticed all this until right after Christmas 1996, when I'd decided to build myself a desk—a desk whose only adornments would be pictures of Nicholas. In my small apartment I stacked wood, stain, varnish, brushes; for about a week I hammered and sanded and brushed. One day in January, when I was taking a break, shirt stripped off, I looked at myself in the mirror. What I saw startled me: a man, not too young any more, covered with sweat and stain and fine sawdust. Okay body, no visible abdominals, torso hairier than the ideal, more functional than pretty. You would never call this man a "boy." To me, he looked amazingly like my father.

In February 1997, when Nicholas was about eighteen months old and I'd settled into this commuting routine, Rose and I started discussing, and occasionally arguing about, when Nicholas should finally be weaned. The force of my own eagerness for this project took me by surprise, and I realized, not without some amusement, that I was fulfilling a classic Freudian role in a situation that was anything but conventional—trying to interpose myself between this child, who was not mine and yet to whom I'd become deeply attached, and its mother, to whose body I had no claims and for which I felt no physical desire. But Nicholas's frequent and contented nursing had begun to irritate me: at some deep and irrational level— and this is what surprised and embarrassed me, who was so profoundly connected to my own mother—I was afraid he'd be a mamma's boy, dependent, incomplete, unlucky. All parenting is probably, and not always unconsciously, profoundly remedial; you compensate for the things you yourself didn't have, and steel yourself against the indulgences you suspect may have spoiled you. Finally Rose and I made a deal: we'd start by trying to eliminate his bedtime nursing. Rose warned me. "You don't realize how difficult it is," she said. "It's so hard to hear him screaming at night and not go in." She wanted to know if I would help out by coming to stay at her place full-time during what we were calling "weaning week." For a moment I experienced the same panicked claustrophobia I've known from dating, from the times when a boy I've been going out with starts insisting that I be in certain places at certain times; but soon the panic passed. This was different. The reason, I told myself, is that I loved Nicholas, and I haven't always loved those other boys, merely wanted them, had them. With a readiness that seemed for once perfectly natural, I said yes.

We didn't need all that time, though. Maybe it was because the two of us were there; maybe not. Whatever the reason, Nicholas gave up his nighttime nursing after one fifteen-minute shrieking jag, the first night, and a four-minute one the next night. I know, because Rose and I timed him as we stood outside his door, gripping each other as he screamed. After that, all we'd need to do was to put him in the crib, kiss him, and he'd be out like a light. On some nights I'd sleep in the bed in his nursery, listening to his breathing, which unlike mine was deep, even, and untroubled.

On a chilly October night in 1996 I emerged from the train station near Rose's house and got into the front seat of the black four-door Volvo that she finally bought a few months after the baby was born. Her previous car was a 1980 Ford that was unsafe for children, to say nothing of adults: although I could never absolutely confirm it, I secretly suspected that small, more or less minor parts of the engine were flying out as we drove at speeds above twenty miles per hour. Although I teased Rose mercilessly about that car, I liked the fact that she found it so hard to let it go: her refusal to give up on things reminded me of something; was, for me, a symbol, a reflection of a deep integrity and authenticity. "You can't keep driving this jalopy," I said one morning over a cup of coffee a few months earlier. "Our lives are meaningless, naturally, but *try* to think of the baby." In the months since Nicholas was born it had become part of our routine for me to make an occasional pronouncement about the kind of things that dads were once supposed to worry about: when and whether to cut the grass or to fertilize, what kind of mutual funds to put Nicholas's college money in, what was the safest kind of car. Rose, who leads a far more orderly life than I do, doesn't really need advice from me, but I think that the ironic enthusiasm with which I played my paternal role allowed her to relax a little, to shrug off the sense of her own huge responsibility, even if only in play. Anyway, she bought the Volvo.

That night, as we drove home, Nicholas, who was then about fifteen months old, was babbling contentedly to himself, probably about the moon. He'd been a late walker, and was just now beginning to utter some recognizable words: "mamma" was a very recent addition. Even with her contacts in, Rose tends to peer at the world like someone very nearsighted; as she cautiously navigated the streets that led to her house, she told me, just as cautiously, about his new vocabulary. Houses passed by, and there was a loaded silence. I knew what was coming; I'd been thinking of it myself for a while.

"You know," she said, carefully, turning into her street and pulling up in front of her house, a narrow three-story brick structure built around 1910, which has an old-fashioned porch swing that always feels as if it's going to rip itself out of the hooks that attach it to the porch roof, but doesn't, "we have to decide soon what he's going to call *you*."

The subject of names had been on my mind, because lately Nicholas had been calling me something that sounded as though it might lie somewhere halfway between Nano and Daddo, and Rose and I, without quite looking at each other, would try to get him to enunciate more clearly, to see, as if we were playing some new variant of Ouija, whether it was a proper name or a proper noun he was trying to say. A few weeks before, I'd talked with a friend of mine, a social worker who handles "special" family situations, and asked her about the name issue. "What's he going to call me?" I asked. I didn't like the idea of his calling me by my first name, and yet anything like "Daddy" was clearly inappropriate, even though I'd been feeling more and more that, in some sense, he was my child—not *my* child, in the sense that he was my own son, but the child in my life, my life's child. My friend listened to me mimicking Nicholas's pronunciation (and it had occurred to me that it was just possible that all he was saying was an elaborate "hello") and finally laughed. "You're stuck halfway between your name and some kind of fatherhood, whether you like it or not," she said. "Which probably just about hits the nail on the head, Mr. Nano-Daddo. You're a hybrid."

There is nothing more elemental, and hence more vulnerable to stress, than our desire to know who we truly are, to know in detail the lineage that created us. It is for this reason that the *Ion,* like many subsequent dramas about secret births and children reunited with their long-lost birth parents, flirts with farce, even as it explores the darker corners of the emotional imagination. Sometimes the farce triumphs; sometimes it's the tragedy. The flip side of the *Oedipus the King,* in a way, is *The Importance of Being Earnest.*

After being told that her husband Xuthus has discovered his long-lost child, Creusa is distraught with jealousy and fear. She believes she will be supplanted back at home, in Athens, the infertile wife of a man who now has a son and heir; worse, she knows how loathed stepmothers are, and recoils from being forced into that role. One of the unhappy woman's servants, a sly and ill-intentioned old man, plays upon her fears and—here is where the balance begins tilting towards tragedy—persuades her to try to assassinate Ion, who is of course, still unbeknownst to her, her own child and not, in fact, her husband's natural son. There is a great deal of business with poisoned potions and birds keeling over after drinking from Ion's cup. Ion is saved—Apollo will not allow his child to die—and for a melodramatic moment seems poised to kill his mother, until, at last, the gods intervene. But it is not, in the end, Apollo, the real father, who saves the day; his priestess, the Pythia, appears just in time to prevent the act of violence, explaining to Creusa and Ion that they are mother and son. As proof, she brings from within the temple the basket in which Ion had been exposed, preserved all these years in anticipation of this day. Ion watches incredulously as the strange Athenian woman in front of him correctly identifies the contents of the basket, proving her own identity. Joyfully, the parent and child are reunited, revealed to each other at last. Still believing that Xuthus is his natural father, an elated Ion takes his newfound mother by the hand, declaring that they must go immediately and share the good news with his father. And now Creusa reveals the final secret: that it is Apollo, in fact, who is his father; Xuthus's belief that he has a son in Delphi, and that Ion is that boy, is a sad delusion fostered by the god for his own ends. "If this is true," Ion asks his mother, "why should Apollo give his son to others? Why say that Xuthus is my father?" "He does not say this," Creusa replies. "You are his son *as a gift* given to Xuthus, just as one might give his own son to a childless friend, to adopt as his own son and heir." This explanation must have seemed natural for the Greeks in Euripides' audience, whose worst nightmare was childlessness—the possibility that your line, your name, might dry up and disappear.

So Ion and Creusa tell Xuthus nothing. He will never know who this boy, the boy he thinks is his son, really is.

When Nicholas was about two and a half, he was obsessed by trucks, lawn mowers, trains, cars—anything, basically, that was loud and moved. *So much for nurture,* Rose and I would say jokingly, around the house. He seemed to be very athletic. Privately, we have ideas of what we'd like him to be like, of course: musical, well read, well rounded; obviously I want him to learn to swim, and Rose had a great-uncle who was a famous fencer. I like the idea of Nicholas learning to fence, because I think fencing is elegant and disciplined. Nicholas, of course, has no notion of these things, and Rose and I are so embarrassed by our secret aspirations, which so clearly reflect our own vanities, that we can't bring ourselves to talk about Nicholas's future except in the form of a joke. For now, at any rate, he's a real *boy*-boy, and he careens around the house saying, "Whee, I'm crashing that truck!" and making loud exploding noises. I suppose that at some point I played with toy trucks and planes—I know we *owned* them—but my mother tells me that I could occasionally be found next door, at the house of the little girl who was my best playmate when I was small, organizing her Barbie show house—a memory I'd buried, no doubt out of shame.

Nicholas loves watching the landscaper Rose hires to cut the grass twice a month, whose name is Charlie. If I'm home—by this I mean, when I am in Rose's home—when Charlie comes to mow the lawn, Nicholas will indicate that he wants me to pick him up, which I do, and we move slowly from window to window throughout the ground floor of Rose's house, all along the side of the house and then into the kitchen, where we can look at the back lawn, watching Charlie cut the grass. Recently, while we were doing this, Nicholas got the still, solemn look he'll get when he's either about to make an important observation, which he does frequently and with great solemnity ("We must *not* waste chocolate"), or about to burst into tears, which he does rarely but apocalyptically. He's grown into an imp-faced, tallish toddler, and can use his many expressions—especially a variation of the under-the-brows one made famous by Princess Diana—slyly, and to great effect. But now he was dead serious. He turned to me, as we watched the man moving up and then down Rose's back lawn, and said—this was in the most distinct, grown-up tone I'd ever heard him use, and with flawless syntax—"I think Charlie is a *great* man because he is pushing that lawnmower all the way across the lawn."

Although I've seen pictures of my grandfather, my mother's father, in bathing suits, I rarely saw his body; in my memories he is always completely and elaborately dressed. He was the only man I'd ever seen, until I went to my Southern college, who wore white shoes. He wore feathers in his hat, feathers that he'd carefully smooth down before donning the hats, and that his last wife—who had watched as another, earlier husband and their fourteen-year-old daughter were sent in one direction, the direction of death and incineration, while she was sent in the other, and who for this reason, perhaps, hated pleasure—would pull out of the hat bands. He was the only man I'd seen who paid attention to his nails, and who wore cologne every day, rather than just for catered affairs. His eyes, which looked to me huge and wet from behind his thick glasses, were the pale oblivious blue of a newborn's. He always wore beautiful pajamas to bed, and told such funny stories that he once made his sister-in-law pee in her pants at the dinner table. He pronounced his *v*'s like *w*'s and vice versa, and became genuinely angry at me one day, when I was home one summer between terms at college, for teasing him about it.

"When I came this country I worked ten hours a day, six days a week, for twelve dollars a week," he said, pronouncing the numeral as *tvolf,* "and then I'd go to night school. So don't tell me how to speak English." When we five children of his only child would misbehave, he'd speak darkly of the great cat-o'-nine-tails he had hidden in his luggage, the one he rubbed with garlic. Once, when I was nine and he caught me setting Matchbox cars on fire behind the apple tree in the backyard, he chased me around the yard wielding a milk bottle, threatening to beat me black and blue. *A fire! A fire! Do you want to kill us all?* he screamed, over and over, and it wasn't until much later that it occurred to me that he might have been thinking of his childhood house in flames in 1916—or, to be precise, the right half in flames, because the Russian shell had completely flattened the left—and of how the water in the river Swica grew hot and began to boil after another shell exploded while he and his mother and brothers and sisters were fleeing the barrage in the night, and of how they all watched as a schoolmate of his was boiled to death in the river beside which they had once picnicked.

He deserved his reputation as a great raconteur. Some of his best stories were based on the lies he'd told or tricks he'd played in order to survive: how he yelled "Fire!" when he and his sister were trying to board the boat to America—this was in Rotterdam, they'd been traveling by train for two weeks—which they were in danger of missing because their pre-embarkation medical exams were taking too long; in the ensuing confusion, he grabbed her hand and they slipped up the gangway. He fancied himself a trickster. When I was thirteen he took me on my first trip to New York City, where he had banking to do: he wanted to move some money into a new CD in order to get a free television set for my mother.

The woman at the bank asked him for his address, and as usual when doing his New York banking, he gave her my parents' address; then she asked for the address of the recipient of the gift, and he gave again the house number and the street name—obviously, a single-family suburban dwelling. The woman looked up and said, with the faked regret of the career clerk, that the free-gift offer wasn't valid if the recipient and the giver of the gift lived in the same household. My grandfather looked at her evenly and said, pointing to the piece of paper in front of her, which she'd begun to crumple, and motioning for her to keep writing, "My daughter lives in Apartment 1. I live in Apartment 3." My mother got the TV.

· When my grandfather told his stories, you would hang on each slowly enunciated sentence without daring to breathe, even though you knew the end because you'd heard it the previous summer when he'd come, and you'd wait for the triumphant conclusion, which he would proffer like a candy:

> So I yelled "Fire!" and in all the confusion we got on the boat, and that's how we came to America.

> But it was too late, and she died a week before the wedding.

When he came to visit us, my mother had to cook special things for him that she never made at any other times: things that were finer and more expensive than what we'd ordinarily eat. He would only eat tiny, tiny peas. He would drink rye whisky from heavy lead-crystal glasses filled nearly to the top and tell racy jokes not only in Polish, for the benefit of my mother's cleaning lady, but in German and Yiddish and Russian and Hebrew. He had a star sapphire pinkie ring, which he was wearing when, shot through with cancer of the bowel and unable anymore to take pleasure in his meals, he jumped into the uselessly small swimming pool of his deluxe apartment complex in Miami Beach, knowing he was too weak to swim. The ring is now in the top drawer of my dresser, and I sometimes take it out and look at it, although I never wear it. My grandfather had been on ocean liners, the passenger lists and menus of which he had carefully saved and would show to me. He spoke six languages, and had four wives.

In this man's family, photographs were of supreme importance, because they were the proof of beauty, and when they'd lost everything else, their house and their land and the brewery and the meat-packing plant and the trucks and the servants and their daughters and their dignity, beauty was what was left. You can see the tremendous force of my grandfather's vanity in his first wedding picture, from 1928, when he married my grandmother, a picture which I now have: the handsome face you see there is that of a young man who means to own one day a suit of evening clothes like the white tie and tails he had to rent to be married in. It is the face of someone who enjoys being known as a ladies' man, and who is so intent on his own satisfactions, perhaps, that he becomes careless. My father, in a bitter moment, told me once a piece of ancient gossip his mother had heard: that in the forties or fifties my mother's father had had a mistress. What my father actually said was that my grandfather had had "a woman friend," and when he told me this I didn't wonder why he was telling me, since by then I was familiar with the elaborate terrains and intricate strategies of my parents' contests with each other, but instead could not get the absurd arch euphemism "woman friend" out of my head, which, because it was so clearly a relic from my father's own lost youth, moved me much more than did the news he'd been saving all those years.

For a long time I assumed that my grandmother, my mother's mother, the one who took me on long walks, had been rather stupid; this, at any rate, is always what I'd heard between the lines of my parents' conversations. My grandfather and his beautiful siblings, I knew, were the clever ones. Like everyone else, my grandmother lived in terror of my grandfather, of his moods and depressions and many exigencies with respect to clothes and food and manners. A few years ago, when my mother showed me some of her mother's recipes, I was surprised to see how forceful and clear my grandmother's handwriting was, and wondered whether she saved her clarity and personality for her cooking, since in my grandfather's presence she was an assenting shadow. I only recently learned that, once when her husband was in a hospital for one of his many surgeries—and not long before she herself died so suddenly—my grandmother had turned to my mother and said, for no apparent reason, "I would divorce that man, but where would I go?"

I used to look at my grandfather, when I was in my teens, and I would think excitedly of his many wives and vacations, his annual trips to the baths in Germany, the many revisions of his will (which always stayed the same anyway), the elaborate funeral plans that he dictated to me when I was fourteen—I would think of these things and would see not a terrible irresponsibility and a self-absorption so complete that it obliterated four wives and one child, but glamour. Then I would think of my father, with his one wife and five children, his poly-cotton shirts and his many interchangeable rep ties, predictable as graphs, his stoic devotion to broken automobiles and to the crosswords and offspring he kept trying to find solutions for, and find him dull.

Of course I wanted to be my grandfather. I was fifteen; I was a child. I wanted to play.

The evening of the day on which Rose had brought up the subject of names, I put Nicholas to bed. He'd been fussy after dinnertime, avoiding me and grabbing onto Rose whenever he could, whimpering and begging to be held. Usually I'd pretend not to mind when he got this way—if I reached out to hold him he'd swing his body abruptly away and fling himself at Rose's legs—but this night it got to me, and I growled a bit as he buried his head in a long black skirt Rose was wearing, as if trying to get back inside her the same way he came out. I made an impatient gesture, and Rose gave me a reproachful look, muttering something about his being overtired. "Fine," I said, taking my revenge, "but *I'm* going to change him and put him to bed." The baby wailed a little as I picked him up and headed upstairs to the bathroom where his changing table is, but by the time I'd diapered and changed him he'd calmed down, staring out the window and looking at the sky.

We went into his room, and I read him *Goodnight Moon,* which we hadn't looked at in a while and which I had assumed he'd outgrown. I hoped he wouldn't want to nurse; tonight, it was important to me to feel that he needed *me.* As I was thinking about how silly and selfish and obvious this was, I noticed that he'd fallen silent. He was lying sprawled in my arms, in the same position he nursed in, his feet sticking out past my right elbow, his head cradled in the crook of my left arm. He was looking right at me, very levelly. It was a weirdly grown-up expression—I felt he was *contemplating* me—but instead of flinching or cooing, I stared back at him, wondering what he was thinking, whether he was wondering what to call me.

After a while his lids started fluttering, and his eyes closed. I could tell from his breathing that he wasn't quite asleep yet—the rise and fall of his small torso was still too tentative. His valentine-shaped nostrils dilated minutely with each breath, and I was struck forcefully by how beautiful he is: not, anymore, because he looked like a Gerber baby model, or indeed like anyone, but because he looked so much like his own self.

We rocked like that for a long time, and then two things happened. First, Nicholas fell deeply asleep. His eyelids were perfectly smooth now, and his breaths came at longer intervals. Second, the anxiety I'd been feeling all day subsided. Something my social worker friend had said that morning kept ringing in my head: *hybrid, hybrid, hybrid.* I looked at Nicholas, and then thought of the beautiful boys I have held at night: the slender dark-haired Southerner who was my boyfriend for two years, the one whom my best friend called "the Willow" and who, because of a particular way he had of pronouncing certain words like "can" and "am" (which he did as though they were spelled "ken" and "em") has made it hard for me to listen to a song called "Losing My Religion"; the handsome German prince who spoke surprisingly bad English, and who would touch the sensitive parts of my body and say, meaning something else, "I see you have many feelings"; many others. I thought of all these boys, and then I looked at Nicholas, and suddenly I realized that in some cases I hadn't loved those other "boys" at all, and in most others hadn't loved them as well as I could or should have. I had thought that loving them meant wanting them, possessing them, and so I had stayed with them as long as they left me alone and whole and untouched—

allowed me to be who I thought I knew I was. None had done what this child, whom I realized I truly loved, had done: challenged me, compelled me to confront the difficult riddle of who I really might be, forced me to choose a new name for myself.

My grandfather drowned himself. They found him one morning floating face down, dressed as always in his pajamas, in the pool behind his building. The medical examiner determined that he had died sometime the night before. It was mid-June in south Florida; the night before had been unbearably hot and muggy. Afterwards, my mother would console herself by saying, sometimes aloud, even if no one was listening, that at least his last sensation had been of the pleasant coolness of the water. Silently, I'd wonder what it was that he saw as he stood by the side of the pool and looked down into the dark water, deciding to die.

It wasn't until I knew Nicholas, was around a child for a long time, that I finally understood why my grandfather married three more times after my grandmother died and before he did.

First he married an Israeli woman who, if my one dim memory of her is correct, once argued about cooking with him, and although there's no way to prove it, I can't be sure that her swift departure from his household and from our lives was not unconnected to her failure to cater to his tastes. That woman was soon followed by a wealthy widow whose requests that he do yard work at her country place were greeted with an aristocratic horror and disdain—aristocratic not in any real sense, of course, but in that other, private sense, the one that had to do with an aristocracy of deep-set eyes and strong jaw-lines and fastidiousness in clothes and the food your wife served you; then, finally, he married the gnarled Russian woman, who had known Auschwitz and who survived him, too, and who at his funeral cried, mysteriously and repeatedly, *Entschuldig' mir, entschuldig' mir*—"Forgive me, forgive me." My father, who prides himself on what I know he privately characterizes as a hardheaded practicality—a quality that he believes I, like my grandfather, lack—my father thinks that my grandfather's last wife cried these words because she killed him. Literally killed him, that is, took him into the elevator and then downstairs, moving him to the side of the pool and pushing him into it, in the dead of that hot night, either at his request or at the bidding of some nameless and unnameable demons of her own.

This is what my father thinks, now that I have translated *Entschuldig' mir, entschuldig' mir* for him. But what I think is this: she wanted forgiveness for outliving him.

I had always ascribed my grandfather's many marriages to the great vanity that even I, who adored him, could not pretend to ignore. Like all vain people, he needed many mirrors, and his many wives, aside from cooking and cleaning and iron-ing for him, also gave him someone to eat and primp and dress up in front of. His vanity, his need to be attended to, also explained his many illnesses and frequent surgeries, the bottles and bottles of pills so numerous that he had a brown calfskin attaché case just for his medications for when he traveled. When he would arrive at my parents' house, we children would line up in the bathroom and watch him take his pills, which he set out with great precision on the bathroom coun-tertop, arranged by color. As vain of his things as he was of himself, he enjoyed orderliness. "Tonight," he would intone, "I think I'll take a blue one and a red one." We giggled. I think he enjoyed having an audience.

But now I see that he kept getting married because he feared death so greatly. To be a lover—to be a desirer, a collector—is to be self-obsessed, for your desire is ultimately about yourself. But to be a parent is, ultimately, to efface yourself—your *self*. I don't think my grandfather ever managed this, which is why he had so many wives but only one child. In our different ways, my grandfather and I are great desirers. When he was still alive I did not know what questions to ask him, and now that he is dead there is no way to interrogate him about these things, the things that hover behind the facts, behind the dates of births and marriages and deaths about which I did interrogate him, behind, even, the stories and tragedies and comedies of family history that he told so brilliantly well. I cannot ask him these things, about why he kept marrying, desiring. But I think I know how he felt. My grandfather must have thought that as long as he could change his mind, always be a lover, make new plans, take new wives, he'd still have a chance, could still cheat death. I think I know what he thought. He must have thought that as long as he maintained the illusion of choice, he would live forever.

Like most examples of the dramatic technique called deus ex machina, the improbable appearance of the goddess Athena, Apollo's sister, at the end of Euripides' *Ion*—an appearance that swiftly and somewhat improbably ties up all the loose dramatic ends, tidying up what has been an extremely messy situation—is less than fully satisfying.

First of all, we are led to expect that it will be Apollo himself, the boy's true father, who will appear and explain everything to the mortal characters; but this god remains elusive, absent, an idea more than an agent. "Apollo did not think it right to come himself, lest he be blamed for what happened in the past," Athena declares, trying (I like to imagine) to hide her own embarrassment and irritation at her libidinous and irresponsible sibling. Athena goes on to declare once and for all what Ion still has trouble believing: that his true, biological father, whom he will never know or see, is a god, and that he, Ion, has been given to an adoptive, mortal father to be reared, so that he might find an established place among men, and inherit the throne of the city he will lead. Disingenuously, perhaps, Athena attributes this tangled story's happy ending to Apollo himself: he made Creusa's labor very easy, she declares, so that the girl's family would not know of the birth; he assigned his brother Hermes to place the child in the Pythia's care, in the temple of Apollo at Delphi, so that the infant would grow up in his real father's house; finally, he engineered the placement of the young boy in the royal house of Athens, under the care of Xuthus, not his real father but a loving, if deluded, father figure.

Like most ex machina appearances, this one leaves the audience, if not the characters themselves, with more answers than questions. There is, of course, the lingering question of Apollo's embarrassment, his refusal even at the very end to show himself to his son—a refusal that suggests he knows his glib libidinousness, the endless succession of Daphnes and Creusas, is wrong, and that the consequences shame him and are not without guilt. And there is, even more, the question of double paternity, the boy with two fathers, Apollo and

Xuthus, the unseen and the seen: on the one hand, the absent immortal who fathered him, giving him his genetic identity, the divine nature that will make him a leader of tribes and nations and civilizations, and, on the other hand, the mortal man who, when all is said and done, will *be there* for the boy, who will watch him grow up, giving to him and guiding him, even if he is not nearly as potent as the secret father the boy knows of, but can never acknowledge or know. Like most tragedies, the *Ion* leaves you not with a pat answer but with a paradox, a *men* and a *de*. At the end of your search for identity, the *Ion* seems to say, your search for true and absolute knowledge of yourself, of your genetic makeup and the traits that make you always and repeatedly and inalienably *you*, there may not be a single answer but instead another riddle, the answer to which is unknowable to everyone but you: that you may be two things rather than one, a boy with two fathers.

In the end, it was Nicholas who came up with the answer to the question of what to call me. Daddo passed pretty quickly, and although he's occasionally achieved something closer to my name—Naniel or Danyo, or something like that—it's been Nanno since he turned two. In terms of absolute precision it's not a huge improvement over Daddo, of course—the middle *n*'s were achieved at the cost of the initial *D* in the earlier version—but he seems comfortable with it. It's something he can say, or yell, easily. It's also something with which Rose and I are both more comfortable than we were with Daddo, which was too close to something known, in the dictionary, and therefore not accurate enough to describe my twofold, hybrid nature.

One morning in the spring of 1998 Nicholas, Rose, and I were all lying in Rose's bed—we tend to assemble there in the morning and Nicholas will tell us about his dreams, which tend these days to be about riding horses—and Nicholas was enthusiastically listing all the people he knew, what their names were and who their parents were. "Who is Mamma's mother?" we asked, and he shouted back, gleefully, "Gramma!" "What is Gramma's name?" "Awice!" "Who is Momma's father?" "Poppa!" "What is Mamma's name?" "Wose!" This went on for some time; we got through most of the kids in his day-care class and a lot of the family, too, with Nicholas shouting each name triumphantly. Then I thought of something. "What is Nanno's name?" I asked. He looked at me carefully, and then laughed and clapped his hands, like the winner on a game show. "Nanno's name is . . . Daniel!!" he said, enunciating it perfectly.

So Nicholas has decided that Nanno is my title, and that that title lies somewhere between my name, which it approximates, and something else, something that he knows isn't my name and the meaning of which he won't know for years to come, although I and some others do. "It does sound like *something,*" Rose's father, who is half-Italian, said, a few weeks after the name game on Rose's bed that morning. Even before he went on to finish his thought, I knew what he was going to say: that "Nanno" was a hybrid, a cross between my proper name and *nonno,* which is the Italian word for "grandfather."

IV. MYTHOLOGIES

Nobody has ever written a tragedy about Ismene, Antigone's sister—the one who counseled caution, the one who lived. How could you? Tragedy loves extremity. It celebrates the vertiginous beauty of total destruction.

If tragedy were, as we sometimes like to think, a theater of the clash between Right and Wrong, it wouldn't be so gripping: its tension derives from something much more complex and interesting, which is the conflict between two Rights. Sophocles' *Antigone,* a play that is, in many ways, the quintessential tragedy, ends with the premature burial of a young girl who, after she is condemned to die by her uncle, the king, refers to herself as a bride of death. The play follows the disastrous career of the children of Oedipus, the ill-fated Theban king whose discovery of his terrible twofold nature—son-husband, brother-father, king-scapegoat, savior-destroyer—is the subject of Sophocles' *Oedipus the King.* The action of the *Antigone* takes place on the day after Oedipus's two sons have killed each other in a battle for the Theban throne. The hero of the *Oedipus the King,* has no idea of who he really is, and spends the play finding out, horribly; the heroine of the *Antigone* knows exactly who she is—what her terrible parentage is, what mythology her disastrous biology destines her for— and, perversely in a way, but also, in the end, inevitably, sets out to prove it at the cost of her own life.

After Oedipus learns his awful secret, his wife-mother, Jocasta, kills herself; as we know, Oedipus blinds himself, dooming himself to a career as yet another of mythology's wise blind men, a man whose hard-won inner sight comes at the price of his eyes. Oedipus retires from the throne that his cleverness had won him, and goes into exile. His two sons—who, because of the incestuous marriage, are also his brothers, two things at once, like Oedipus himself—his two sons, Polynices and Eteocles, agree to a rotating kingship: each will reign for one year, allowing the other to take over at the end of that year. This arrangement doesn't last too long, of course, sibling rivalry being what it is. There comes a time when Eteocles refuses to step down at the end of his turn at being king; his brother Polynices flees Thebes for Argos, where he marries into the Argive king's family and, with six fellow warriors, plots an invasion of Thebes. Polynices' invasion is finally repelled by the Thebans fighting under Eteocles, but only after bitter bloodshed. During the climactic battle at the walls of Thebes, the two brothers deliver mortal blows to each other at precisely the same moment.

Here is where the action of the *Antigone* begins. Creon, the brother of Oedipus's wife-mother, Jocasta, the uncle (and great-uncle) of the blind man's children, takes control of the city. His first edict as king concerns the disposition of the bodies of the two fallen brothers. Eteocles, who defended the city, will receive a splendid state funeral, while Polynices' body will be thrown to the dogs "unburied and unwept"; anyone caught attempting to offer him funeral rites will be stoned to death. Antigone ignores her sister Ismene's admonitions to lie low and avoid trouble; she goes to the place where her brother's unburied body lies and sprinkles it with a few token handfuls of dirt, a few ritual drops of water, thereby upholding both religious law and family duty. But in so doing she violates the edict of her uncle, King Creon, who believes above all in the primacy of law. Antigone is caught and condemned to die— not by stoning, after all, a fate presumably beneath the dignity of a princess of the royal line, but by being buried alive in a rocky cave. The fierce adolescent princess who sees no choice other than to hear her own conscience, who insists on the primacy of family ties above all things, would likely have lived, in some other, nontragic universe, a universe of forgiveness and compromise in which her opponent wasn't bound to be as convinced of the justice of his case as she was of hers. A universe, in other words, where *men* and *de* were continuous rather than implacably opposed. In this quintessential tragedy, the only character who counsels compromise—and, therefore, life—is Ismene. "You have a warm heart for cold matters," Ismene tells her death-obsessed sister at the beginning of the play when she, Ismene, declines to assist in the forbidden burial. But it is she, ultimately, who leaves her sister, and us, cold.

The protagonists of so many tragedies are extraordinarily young: Antigone, *Bacchae*'s Pentheus, Hippolytus in the play that goes by his name but which is far more famous in Racine's adaptation, *Phèdre* (the Greeks were interested in the chaste youth; the French, in the erotomane woman). All are, essentially, adolescents. The extreme youth of these heroes, and the greater age of the antagonists who often seek to thwart them, suggests another conflict that subtends tragedy's elaborate geometries of principle, action, and self-destruction: the conflict between the fierce absolutism of youth and the compromises necessary for maturity. It is the beauty of dead youth that we remember when we leave the theater, the beauty of those for whom there was, finally, no alternative but to die, to forfeit life for its opposite. Compromise cannot be tragic; it leaves no residue to remember afterwards. The Athenians in their eulogies of the war dead spoke of a thing called *thanatos kalos,* "beautiful death"—a death that is beautiful in part because it preserves you in memory, in the oration in which you are being remembered, as pure potential, so that your death becomes, in a way, a means of ensuring intact beauty, a monument to itself. In the *Antigone,* if the heroine can go to her execution singing that she is a "bride of Hades," a bride of death, it is because, had she chosen life, married, become a real bride, there would have been no story to tell, nothing to celebrate, nothing to sing. The everyday is anathema to tragedy. Out of self-annihilation, out of failure and lack and destruction, tragedy builds the beautiful monument that is itself.

We go to tragedies because we are ashamed of our compromises, because in tragedy we find the pure beauty of absolutes, a beauty you cannot have if you choose to live. You can't make a tragedy out of survival. You can't write a tragedy about Ismene.

Why would you erect a monument that was a lie?

The cemetery where three generations of my mother's family lie buried is on the southern part of a necropolis that spreads east from Brooklyn through to Queens. It's a fifteen-minute drive from midtown Manhattan, when the traffic is light, but of course when the first of those ancestors died, in 1923—when the girl I am going to be telling you about, the one with the lying tombstone, died gasping on a narrow bed in Lenox Hill Hospital—the trip probably took a good deal longer. When, as a child, already obsessed by her story, I would ask my grandfather about this, he would say that there had been horses with black trappings; but of course that could be some other memory. His other sister, in old age, insisted to me that she had watched as Emperor Franz Josef's son Rudolf (of *Mayerling* fame) rode up the steps of the city hall in Lemberg, the provincial capital, on a white horse, and neither I nor anyone else ever managed to tell her that this dead prince had in fact shot himself a decade before she was born. So the horses caparisoned in black could be some other, older memory—perhaps of his father's funeral, in 1912—the wrong memory seeping into the one I was asking for. Or perhaps it was just another lie. Slow-stepping horses plumed with jet makes for a better story than a rented black car puffing on a highway.

Now there are no horses, only the occasional car speeding on what used to be the Interboro Parkway but, as I found out recently when I got lost as I went there to visit her, has been renamed for a dead baseball player. The road, all speed and horizontality, abuts the back fence of Mount Judah, which is absolutely still and composed of nothing but mute verticals. It is against that fence that she lies buried, at the back of the section marked out for Jews who came from Bolechów.

The largest and most grandiose plot in this section, a plot that has small stone benches for visitors to sit on and, I imagine, think about their secrets, is my family's plot. In the center of this expanse of ground stands an imposing gray slab, like a headstone but much larger, fitted with delicately wrought bronze Art Nouveau mountings, that bears bronze letters spelling out my great-grandmother's maiden name. This is the name—it would have been the girl's married name, had she lived another week (or so we were told)—this is the name of her first cousins, who paid for her funeral and who, according to my grandfather, were responsible for her death. This stone is low, and you have to be in the cemetery to see it, and so to read it. But you can see her stone, that tall slab of granite sculpted, redundantly, into a dead tree, from the highway.

Once you are inside, the sense of a stone garden yields to an awareness of green: rectangle after manicured rectangle of brisk springy ivy above each grave. The ivy that covers her grave is still clipped every few weeks, seventy-five years after she died, twenty-five since anyone who could actually have known her stopped to leave a stone on top of the granite marker. The ivy is always green; in the center of the rectangle a rosebush, a distant descendant of the one they planted there in 1923, pushes out its flowers every spring, past the unseeing eyes of her photograph, which stares straight ahead, right at you, and smiles. Incongruously, an electric-blue sticker affixed to the stone says PERPETUAL CARE in white letters. My grandfather, her brother, told me that they paid seven hundred fifty dollars for the service back then, when she died—a huge sum of money at the time, which still yields an annuity in a meticulousness that nobody notices. Someone loved her that much, or at least wanted strangers to think so. So maybe PERPETUAL CARE is another small bit of writing on that stone that isn't a lie.

After a year or two in the earth there's little left of you; less after ten; and after thirty, forty years, you simply disappear—not even your bones remain. So she isn't really even there anymore, the young woman who, my grandfather often told me when I was small, died a virgin, died at twenty-six, a young woman who lies now underneath a rock bearing an inscription that is a lie. Everything that she was—the girl with the clear brow and lustrous hair; the girl with the haunted gray eyes that had watched, one morning, as her handsome father rose from their table at a spa in a country that no longer exists, only to fall down dead; the ill young woman with colorless lips that smiled from a sweat-soaked bed, smiled since of course how could she know that this would really be the end of everything, not just the end of this visit, on this late August day, but of herself, her seeing the visitors, smiling at them, her being afraid, everything?; then merely an ugly thing buried out of the sight of the living, an object never a subject, a mass settling back into earth as the flesh failed, the ligaments dissolved and let go, finally, of what they had been made to hold together, the intricate bones of her beautiful face rocked apart, strangers to each other—everything that she had been has, finally, become indistinguishable from the dirt into which they lowered her on a stifling September day so long ago that people born after she died have grown up, led their lives, and died in old age since then. What she is now is none of these things: not the girl, not the young woman, not the sick woman, not the corpse, not the dust; she is just the memory of them, the story about her that I heard from my grandfather and that I in turn will tell others.

Anyway, it was never she I sought, really, never that girl or that woman or even that thing beneath. It was the monument that fascinated, the tree fashioned of rock, the porcelain photograph of the girl with her secret smile, the stone and its undulating Hebrew, the hieroglyphs that seemed, in their curls, also to smile and to say, You cannot know. It is the monument we are looking for when we go there—when I go, I should say, because everyone who knew her is long dead, laid down in the same earth with their own mysteries. Everything here stands *for* her now. Even the patch of ivy is, in its way, symbolic, far too small to cover the human body for which, I suppose, it is meant to serve as a coverlet. I know this because I have gone there and lain down next to it.

Her name had been Rachel, *Ruchel,* but when she came here they gave her a name they thought was more English: Ray. Rae. The spellings varied, as did many spellings in my family's history. *J*'s became *y*'s, *h*'s were lost and mysteriously recovered, the faint dusting of an umlaut—illegal here, in America, something you had to surrender at the immigration desk along with your pride, perhaps, and everything you'd had and been, your easy life of servants and picnics and spas— vanished, sometimes replaced by *e*'s, sometimes not. In the old cemetery in Brooklyn you can see, on five tombstones bearing the German name Jäger, which means "Hunter" and which was their name, four different spellings: Jager, Jaeger, Yager, Yaeger. In the country they had come from, the country that no longer exists, they had been one thing for many centuries; here, they had become many names in the course of one year, the year that separated the old life from the new. In cultures where self-invention is possible, there are always competing versions of names, of stories.

Her name, when she was born, had been Rachel, but on the false monument it is preserved as Ray. There is no record of her birthday, but we know that she was twenty-six late in the summer of 1923, when she died, and so we know, too, that she was eighteen in 1915, when she left the small town where they had always lived and, alone, took a train halfway across Europe to the city where the boat was, and boarded the boat that took her to New York and her mother's rich brother and his fat wife and their four children and their restaurants and the factory that made trimmings and braids for lampshades and upholsteries, the rich ornaments called passementerie, a word I and my siblings knew at an early age, because it was a detail in this story, the story of how we became who we are.

So she is eighteen in one of the rare pictures we have of her, the oldest image of her, one of only three, the one that was taken soon after she arrived. In this picture she poses on a sepia sidewalk with one of the ill-favored rich cousins, and it is this careless snapshot, rather than the studied, finely detailed image that stares at you from her gravestone, that gives you a sense, finally, of how beautiful she must have been. Just like those shadowed eyeless sockets of ancient statues, which can often seem to look at you more profoundly than do those whose stone-chip eyes remain, so here, too, the smudges of shadow on the oval face in this crumbling photograph suggest rather than demonstrate the fine hollows under the high cheeks, and tell you enough to know that the eyes were deepset, even though you can't see the eyes themselves. The hair is pulled back tight against the well-shaped skull: a streak of white is the glare of the 1915 sun. She is smiling, not secretly, as in the other picture, but broadly, a girl's—maybe a country girl's—fresh smile. The cousin who is standing next to her in this picture, pinched into ill-fitting boots with rows and rows of hard little buttons, and buttoned into a too-tight coat, looks faded, failed, old enough to be the raven-haired girl's mother although in truth she is not much older. This woman—the sister of the man whom, my grandfather used to tell me, they would later force Ray to marry—would live to be a very old lady, and lies buried in the big plot, too, about fifteen yards— what do you say? south? below?—her always young cousin. I had lunch with the old lady's son last summer. He is a small man with the family's fine bones, and is now four times as old as my great-aunt was when someone took that picture.

We grew up, my four siblings and I, hearing the story of this beautiful dead girl. It was clear to us from the way that my grandfather told this story that it was richer, more tragic, more unbearably sad than the stories other families could tell. Part of this, of course, was the dead girl's beauty, but most of the exceptional quality of the story had to do with the timing, the fact that she died right before her wedding. *A week before her wedding*. The phrase, even, has a certain lilt, the rhythm of literature rather than life. It couldn't be more dramatic if you were making it up.

So this special girl got her special narrative, and because of these things we were meant to feel that we too were special, the heirs of a tragic but also beautiful narrative. Later, when I was growing up and would wonder why my four siblings and I did not do, were perhaps discouraged from doing, the things that so many of our friends did—listening to pop music, staying out, partying, smoking cigarettes or pot, going away for spring break, buying clothes with logos, doing badly in school, getting our hair cut at the fashionable unisex salon in the new mall instead of the ancient Italian barbers near the A&P, going steady, going on dates—I sensed, without being able to articulate why, that the reason had something to do with the dead girl. When your history is marked by high tragedy and beautiful narratives, not holding yourself apart, allowing yourself to be like the others, is felt as a betrayal.

. . .

Ray was not the first Jäger to come to the States, merely the first to stay. Her older brother, Sam, the oldest, after whom my older brother is named, had come before the war, after the father had fallen over that morning in 1912 and died while taking the healthful waters at the spa in Jaremcze. The oldest brother had come to see whether America was a place that he, as head of the family, might be interested in settling; after a brief visit with the rich cousins, he decided it was not. America was too big, he said, and he'd admitted that he'd rather be a big fish in a smaller pond, so he shook his rich uncle Abe's hand and got back on a boat for Rotterdam, where he took a train through Berlin and on into what by then had become Poland, and returned to the small town where these Jägers had lived for centuries, building their business and marrying well, a smallish place where, in time, he grew rich himself, the biggest man in town, so big that he was at the top of the list that the Nazis, always meticulous, would prepare thirty years after he'd decided against America; and when in the autumn of 1941 the Germans entered Bolechów, they knew exactly where to find him and his wife, the slim beauty with the marcelled hair whose maiden name meant "Snow-light" and who had gotten fat over time, sleek with a surfeit of comfort that all of her apotropaic complaining couldn't quite hide. So they found him easily, he and his wife and their four beautiful daughters, my mother's cousins who would have been old ladies now, whose names no one knows anymore, and whom the Germans had not just killed but raped, my mother once told me as she and I left a Yizkor, a Remembrance, service in 1973. She and I were slowly making our way down the shallow steps of a synagogue that had been meticulously built to conform to the dimensions of the original Temple in Jerusalem, and which years after this conversation took place was demolished to make way for a "townhome community." On the day that she told me this, the October sun was bright and cool, and my mother, who was wearing jet earrings that swung against her high, almost Eskimo cheekbones, told me almost absently, in a way that suggested that this was, in its way, just a story to her, too, a story that was, ultimately, about strangers, that the Germans had raped the four daughters, her beautiful cousins, before they shot them all.

This conversation took place in 1973, the year I'd been bar mitzvahed, the day that the Yom Kippur War in Israel began. My grandfather had another brother, an easygoing man with a sly sense of humor, who had lived a long life because he'd had no notion of being a big fish in a small pond. In the early thirties he had left his hometown, too, and emigrated with his fiery Zionist wife to Palestine. As my mother and I walked in the parking lot of the synagogue and talked of her dead cousins that day, her living cousins—the children of this man, who was recently dead—were at war. Their mother, my great-aunt by marriage, was alive, a tiny beaked woman, still fiery but very ancient now, and one day she would write to me her own version of what happened when the Nazis came to Bolechów. She would write that they took Sam's wife and three of the girls to the camps, and later shot Sam and the eldest daughter, who had fled to the hills and fought with the partisans. (This was the letter in which she'd carefully, almost apologetically, added the word "beautiful" to her description of the dead girls.) But there is another version, a third version, that I have heard from another cousin, in which the Germans shot no one, merely put them on the trains, no different from, no more special than, anyone else. I have also heard that my mother's uncle and aunt and four cousins had been in hiding in the home of their Polish maid when they were betrayed—by another Jewish family, who hoped, by so doing, to win favor for themselves. But then, someone else once told me that they were betrayed by the Polish maid herself, while they were hiding in the basement of Jewish neighbors. There are, as I have said, conflicting versions. Naturally, I preferred the version in which they were handed over by the other Jews: if they were betrayed by their Jewish friends, their deaths, however they may have finally happened, become part of a story about fear and selfishness and a kind of tragic naiveté; the second version is flatter, more obvious, less textured.

So Sam went back—to his ambitions, to a war that, as late as 1939, he never dreamed would touch him, him with his slaughterhouses and trucks and double-breasted overcoats with the fur collars and his money and Polish shiksas to run the house. When my grandfather finally died, after years of meticulous preparation, we found an old wallet among his things: a great smooth rectangle of leather meant for a breast pocket of a man's suit. Carefully folded into this wallet were a number of letters, almost transparent with age and with rereading. These were Sam's final letters to his brother. Apparently my grandfather had carried them in his wallet all those years, feeling them, maybe reading them every now and then, though of course after a few readings he would have had them memorized: I do. The letters are written in an old-fashioned German in an elegant if somewhat impatient hand, the writing of a businessman whose early upbringing and education had not, perhaps, been without pretensions. The earlier ones are filled with minor irritations, business problems, the costs of repairing some company trucks. But by the last one, dated September

1939, he is wondering whether maybe he should write to President Roosevelt—*Roosiwelt*—and try to get a visa for the girls? My mother tells me, recently, that she remembers hearing her father and his sisters talking about money late at night, about the American dollars that, Sam writes in his final letters, are necessary for securing immigration papers, talking after they'd thought the children were asleep, debating whether they had enough to send to Sam, something to help him get out. I wonder now if they decided that they couldn't afford to help, and that more than love or sorrow it was guilt, a terrible and unimaginable guilt, that made my grandfather carry those letters so close to his heart all those years, silently. My mother said that after the war, when people started to learn about what had happened to the Jews of Poland, they would sit at the kitchen table, after school, she and her mother and her father, waiting for news. Then one day she came home from school, and there was a letter on the table, opened, not from Sam, and her father was sitting at the table and crying.

Sam had rejected America, had gone back to Europe, because he wanted to succeed. But Ray, his younger sister, who perhaps had no ambitions, stayed, and in staying saved the rest of them.

I should say, of us.

How do we get from the radiant girl in the small snapshot on that shining day in 1915, a picture whose lower right-hand corner, the part that would have showed her legs, is gone (and it is impossible to think of her with legs, she is always just the immobile torso and the carefully posed, monumental head)—how do we get from the vivid, living girl of 1915, a girl capable of smiling, to the somber statuesque beauty of the formal portrait of 1922, the one meant to commemorate an engagement and used, not too much later, to adorn a tomb?

It was, my grandfather would always say whenever he told me this story, an arranged marriage: a cruelty necessitated by war, poverty, weakness, envy, desire, greed. My grandfather's father—the father of Sam and of Ray, my mother's grandfather and the grandfather of the four raped and murdered cousins, a man of some means, handsome, courtly, goateed—died suddenly in 1912. He was forty-seven. It was after this that his oldest child, Sam, went to the States to check things out, see if the family could live there; made his bad decision; returned home. Then came the First World War. The house and property were destroyed; money ran out; the family became poor. After the war was over, it became clear to my great-grandmother, widowed at thirty-six with seven children, that they could not stay. Impoverished, she appealed to her brother, Abe, long established in America and now quite prosperous, with his restaurant and his factory that made passementerie, for help. Uncle Abe agreed—and here my grandfather would pause, my heart thrumming with the pleasure of a good narrative, waiting for the familiar words that signaled the leap from history into myth—rich Uncle Abe agreed on one condition: that his sister's eldest daughter, Ray, marry his second son, Sam. As in a Greek myth, the price of liberty was a virgin sacrifice, an ugly act smoothed over by the rhetoric of self-interested men, of the self-interested fathers and, sometimes, uncles. Ray, shrewd Uncle Abe observed, had come in 1915, lived with him and his fat wife and children for five years. The match would not seem out of the ordinary to anyone who cared to pry. Wasn't it natural that two young people, two cousins who'd come to know each other intimately over several years, should marry?

So it may have seemed to Abe, but to another Abe—my grandfather—the idea was abhorrent. His sister Ray was beautiful; cousin Sam was—of course, as in all fairy tales—tiny, hunched, bespectacled, scarred by smallpox. My vain grandfather saw no match here. Instead he could only see envy, and a grotesque attempt to buy beauty. "It broke Grandma's heart," he would say as he told and retold this story, his farsighted Mr. Magoo eyes shining hugely behind powerful lenses. "It broke her *heart*." And his voice would turn phlegmy with emotion, and he'd tap his chest, to the left of the sternum, twice. By "Grandma," of course, he didn't mean my grandmother, his wife, but *his* mother; the slip suggested how often he'd told this story to his daughter, my mother, the one whose grandmother's heart had been broken by this enforced alliance. He stabbed the bland suburban air between us with a horny finger for emphasis. "But what could she do? We had *nothing*."

If a bargain had been struck, it was probably soon after the end of the war—sometime in 1919, or perhaps early 1920. The emigrations, at any rate, began in November 1920. The first to come were my grandfather, who would have been eighteen then, and his middle sister—the one who thought she'd seen Prince Rudolf, the one who insisted to me, in a letter written in the spring of 1978, when she was eighty, that she was the ugly one, that compared to the oldest sister, beautiful and dead at twenty-six, and to the youngest, beautiful and dead, twenty years later, at thirty-five, she was nothing, she who had lived to be an old, old lady who had married, had had a child. Yet what is strange about these protestations is that it is quite clear from photographs that this middle sister was, in fact, quite pretty, not perhaps as gravely statuesque as the eldest, nor as translucently delicate as the youngest, but certainly pretty. In a handful of snapshots taken soon after her arrival in the States—taken on top of a loft building on West Twenty-sixth Street in Manhattan, a block from where I now live, that housed the cousins' passementerie factory, the factory where she and my grandfather worked fourteen-hour days, the factory my grandfather would later buy out in an act of long-delayed revenge against the hated cousins for whom he blamed the deaths of his two sisters, forced to marry their son—in pictures taken in 1920 you see the family features: the deep-set blue eyes, a small regular nose, pursed Cupid's bow lips. A pretty face, intelligent, the lips curled downwards perhaps just a bit with a middle child's sour awareness of the essential injustice of things. But pretty. I think now that she only thought she was ugly because she lived, because unlike them she didn't have a classically tragic narrative, didn't have a beautiful death, had lived long enough to outgrow her youth and prettiness.

Two years after my grandfather and this "ugly" one came, there followed their mother, my great-grandmother, and her two youngest, a boy of eighteen and a girl of fourteen, the girl who would also die too young. Everyone was now in New York City. It was time (my grandfather would say at this point in his narrative) to pay up.

The wedding was scheduled for the spring of 1923. As I write this I am looking at the strangest kind of document: an invitation to an event that never took place. An invitation to the beautiful girl's wedding, engineered by her greedy uncle. Flaked and browned with age, it was preserved by my grandfather, along with certain other artifacts—his birth certificate, those desperate letters his brother Sam wrote late in 1939 as the world locked down around him, the small photograph of my grandmother at age six that was used to advertise a certain photographer's establishment on Clinton Street, in the Lower East Side—he kept these things in a box that still smells yeasty with decades of dust and mildew. The front of the invitation is elaborately lettered in Gothic characters, which to me now seem poignant, fancy lettering intended to lend dignity to a sordid occasion. There is my great-grandmother's name, above that of her brother and his wife, a formidable unsmiling woman always and forever known as Tante; the standard words of invitation; the names of the couple, Ray and Samuel; then the date, Monday, May 28th, 1923; the time, 7:30 p.m.; and the location. This information is given again, in Yiddish, on the back of the invitation. In the Yiddish version, the word "Mrs." is merely transliterated into Hebrew characters— *mem-res-samek*—and the transliteration, whenever I read it, reminds me of my early, secretive renderings of English into my other exotic alphabets: Egyptian, Greek.

As a child and later as a teenager, I would sneak into the locked cabinet where these old family documents were kept, sealed away by my mother in plastic bags within creamy manila envelopes, and I would look at this invitation and feel shock— shock that there was nothing here, in the tangible, official record, that betrayed the high emotion and low resentments that had generated this union, this Greek narrative of family desperation and virgin self-sacrifice. I had somehow expected that the greed and jealousy and cruelty that underlay the real story—or what I then believed to be the real story—would somehow inscribe themselves on this piece of paper, bleeding onto it, becoming as visible as the ornate black characters. But like the inscription on the bride's gravestone, the invitation to the wedding that never took place is surprisingly bland, undramatic. It keeps its secrets.

When not properly treated, strep throat can lead to serious and occasionally deadly complications, causing rheumatic fever, weakening the heart. The strep throat that my great-aunts had in the early years of the century was not treated properly. At some point in the spring of 1923—in April, according to my grandfather, the month I was born—Ray became seriously ill. My mother recalls having seen, in her girlhood that was haunted by the photographic presence of so many dead relatives, engraved cards announcing the postponement of the wedding, due to the bride's illness, until the second week of September of that year. Although we have the wedding invitation, which has the fatal glamour of such documents, to my knowledge no copy of this postponement announcement survives. Perhaps my mother merely imagined it.

What is extant is the tombstone, which says that she died on the third of September. There is a Hebrew inscription, and an English inscription, but the English is not in fact a perfect translation of the Hebrew. The English says:

IN MEMORY OF

MY BELOVED

DAUGHTER

AND OUR DEAR

SISTER

RAY JAGER

DIED SEPT. 3, 1923

AGE 26 YEARS

The fiancé and his family, the rich cousins who, according to my grandfather, actually paid for the stone, are left out of the constellation of the bereaved. I used to find the abbreviation

"Sept." disappointingly informal, when I visited this grave as a child, and would wish they'd written out "September."

The Hebrew inscription stands above the English text and directly below the oval portrait. What it says is:

> TO THE MEMORY OF AN UNMARRIED GIRL
> RACHEL DAUGHTER OF ELKANA
> DIED ON 22 ELUL
> IN THE YEAR 5683

Ha'betulah, an "unmarried girl." The word rang in my head the last time I went to this cemetery to visit her, accompanied by an ash-blond boy with blue eyes so pale they seemed, in certain lights, to be transparent, like the eyes of an Arctic dog. This blond boy, who was from Texas, was a boy whom I'd met and dated and run away from, as we so often do when these boys we meet in bars or at dinners or on-line seem, after the sex is over, to want to get close, and then months or a year or two afterwards we can finally become friends, eat with them and take them on strange errands to visit the graves of dead beautiful girls, but only after the embarrassed knowledge that we've used them has faded. I am standing in front of her grave reading the Hebrew to him and this word, *ha'betulah,* is ringing in my head, reminding me of something, and a few days later I realize what it is, a word in a Hebrew text I have been studying, something I am to read at a wedding the following weekend. The wedding is for a young couple whom I know and who want me to read from the Song of Songs. The word is *habatselet,* which in its Hebrew lettering, with the exception of one letter, looks nearly identical to *ha'betulah,* an unmarried girl, a virgin—especially if you've read the latter word on a very old and weathered stone. When I read the stone I see *ha'-*

betulah but think, at first, that it is *ḥabatseleṭ,* a rose of Sharon, a flower like the one that grows out of the earth that is now indistinguishable from her body.

The second verse of the Song of Songs, a text which is alternatively described as an erotic poem and an allegory about the specialness of the Jewish people, of their relationship to God, is *ani ḥabatseleṭ ha'Sharon,* "I am the rose of Sharon." The story of this dead girl, *ha'betulah,* who has long since grown into a rose, *ḥabatseleṭ,* also combines the erotic and—what shall I call it?—the nationalistic; it, too, is an allegory about distinctness and difference. The English inscription signals her virginity by giving her maiden name, Ray Jager, but this isn't quite the same as *calling* her "unmarried." The maiden name implies that she died unwed; but *ha'betulah* asserts, literally carves in stone, the one thing about this girl that would become inscribed in history, through generations of oral narrative as well as in this official, written, even *carved* tradition (the incised inscription, the engraved invitations): that she died unmarried, a virgin, a week before her wedding.

Ha'betulah/ḥabatseleṭ, the virgin and the rose. The rose grows out of the virgin's grave, signaling her difference, her specialness, flowering year after year above the drab ivy that everyone else in this garden of stone receives. Unlike them, she gets a rose: Unlike, for instance, Helen Katz, who lies next to her and who was also born in Bolechów, a girl also dead too young, at twenty-five, in May of 1924. There is an oval portrait photograph on Helen Katz's stone, too, but there is a difference. The difference between Helen Katz and Ray Jager is one you can see in their pictures. Helen looks like a living girl, and Ray, in that oval picture, already looks like a memory; unlike Helen, who is clearly a serious girl sitting in a photographer's studio on a specific day in a specific year, a person in history, Ray smiles at you from within her own myth. And so, unlike the others, Ray gets a flower, something that marks her out, not a normal bride—a virgin who found a husband or for whom a husband was found, a fiancée who got married and had children and died—but a bride of death, a girl who turned a wedding into a funeral, and so, in the myth that was her legacy to her family, to me, fused beauty and loss, glamour and unhappiness, so that they became, in the end, indistinguishable.

So it is not of my beautiful happy friends that I think when I read the Song of Songs that Saturday afternoon, but of the girl whose premature death gave a strange gift to my family, the gift of rich narrative and long-lived myths that, because they signal your difference, is thought to be worth the price, which is death.

Ha'betulah/ḥabatselet, the dead virgin and the living rose . . .

I will never marry; and yet because of this story I have always been fascinated by weddings, since for me the wedding is, above all, the event that might not take place, the thing that can be about tragedy and death as much as it is about happiness and life. When I first began investigating my family history, I would write to old great-aunts and -uncles and demand pictures. *Wedding* pictures were best, I'd tell them, greedy for beauty. In my mind, the wedding picture was the definitive picture: this, after all, is when people looked their most beautiful, most elaborately dressed. How else would you want to be remembered? Of all the pictures that might be taken of you during the course of your life, which might be long, the wedding picture—as posed, formal, and iconic as the photograph on my great-aunt's tomb—was for me the one that represented what you truly looked like.

I have read from the Song of Songs at three weddings. The most recent was the one that took place a week after my last visit to the cemetery. *Shir ha'shirim asher li'Shlomo,* I said loudly from the lectern in an ornate Gothic church, taking my friends by surprise, since even the people I know well think of me more as a student of classical languages than as a Jew who knows Hebrew, *The song of songs,* I repeated, in the unnatural, beautiful syntax that the scholars employed by King James have bequeathed to us as our model of hieratic diction, *The Song of Songs, which is of Solomon*—Solomon, Solomon, the name rang in my head, I know it well, Hebrew *Shlomo,* Yiddish *Schloimele* . . .

A few months earlier, in the middle of winter, I'd read from this same text, this Song of tragic distinction. I'd been invited to read it, this time in Greek, in the modern Greek translation of the poet George Seferis. Seferis did not know Hebrew; he worked from the classical Greek translation of the Bible known as the Septuagint, which is Latin for "seventy"— a reference to the seventy Greek-speaking Jewish scholars who in the third century B.C. translated the Hebrew Old Testament into Greek, since by then the Jews of Alexandria were so assimilated, so Hellenized, that they could not read Hebrew and were in danger of losing completely their cultural identity, the thing that made them special, chosen. This ancient Greek version was the version Seferis translated, and so I was really performing a translation of a translation, a Hellenization of the original Hebrew, and so a perfect reading not only for this particular couple, my Jewish brother and his Greek wife, but for me, too, I who have always migrated back and forth between pagans and Hebrews. "What does Athens have to do with

Jerusalem?" the minister had asked at the beginning of the service, quoting a Greek-speaking church father and evoking
some nervous and some relieved laughter from a congregation
less comfortable with the shadows, the spaces in between, than
we in my family have always been.

The first time I'd read the Song of Songs at a wedding—
this would have been about 1987, on a green hill overlooking a
farm near my college—it was only in English, again in the
King James translation. This first wedding was one I'd thought
would never take place.

The groom was a man I had known during my senior year
in college. He had pale orange hair and skin so fair that fatigue
or stress bruised it like a physical blow. We'd met while learning
to play bridge at a big antebellum house outside of town. The
house, always referred to as the Big House, with its grand por-
tico of eight Ionic columns and its lakes and its follies and its
swimming pool, which you only reached by means of a long
slate-paved walkway infested with poisonous copperheads,
belonged to a woman we both knew, a woman who liked gay
men. The college boys she gathered around her had the good
looks and secret smiles of boys who liked other boys. (Smiles
like that of the tall dark boy, the one who'd stuffed wet fruit
into my mouth while waiting to seduce me, and who was to
die, later, blind and insane, surrounded by the members of the
church choir he had played for, of whom he had seduced
many. During the long days of his dying some of them would
come to visit him, and we'd wonder who they were really
weeping for.) We spent those summer months moving around
the high hot rooms of the old lady's house, seeking coolness,
drinking old wines from her cellar, a coterie of pretty twenty-
one-year-olds flushed with the consciousness that in this
moment, here in July of 1981, drinking this bottle of Yquem

with these hot dry scratchy raspberries in the presence of this brilliant and girlish old woman who'd been baby-sat by Dietrich and Sara Murphy, the lives we were leading just then perfectly mirrored our secret fantasy of who we were meant to be: rarefied, different, exceptional.

I can't remember the names of all the other boys, although I remember their faces and, in a few cases, their smells and the taste of their mouths. I have heard that, except for me and the red-haired boy, they have all died. There was a handsome Kentuckian with gray eyes whose death, a very bad one, perhaps the worst, was described to me in some detail in a letter I opened while sitting in an ugly concrete hotel in Delphi, on a balcony overlooking the valley in which is located the road leading to the triple crossroads at which Oedipus is said to have killed his father. There was the boy who'd waited tables at a restaurant in our college town during the summers between semesters, a slender bony Southern boy, rather handsome despite a beaked nose, mad for show tunes, which he would sing while sloshing crêpe batter along the sides of hot pans, whom I last saw hobbling through the restaurant on what I suppose was his farewell visit, using a walker, wearing huge thick glasses that no one had suspected he'd needed because in health, in his vanity, he wore contact lenses. There was a dancer with blond hair and striking black brows, a boy so much more beautiful than I that I thought he was playing a joke on me when he started to run his warm foot up and down my bare calf under the bridge table one June afternoon at the Big House, while we were drinking sweet wine and eating raspberries from the back lawn, while Chouky yelled at me, really yelled at me with the unfeeling exasperation of a professional, for bidding stupidly; that boy I saw, unexpectedly, in a hospital where I was visiting another dying boy—someone, I kept telling myself, whom I'd had sex with only once—but of course by then he didn't recognize me because by then he couldn't see. As I passed his room I heard the nasal drawl of rural Virginia coming from the people around him, and remembered that he'd come from someplace called Emporia, the Greek etymology of which I'd begun to tell him as we walked home on the night of the stupid bidding to his place along a road that had, I'm fairly sure, the word berry in its name.

Those were some of the boys I knew that summer. Only I survived, I and the tall boy from the famous Richmond family, pale skinned and wide jawed and grave, his red hair cut so short for the summer heat that you could see the whitish scalp beneath it, a small blood vessel that I couldn't stop looking at pulsing under the bluish skin at the hollow of his throat . . .

This is all I can say about him; what is important is that he got married. "I'm getting married," he told me on the phone, years after that summer, years during which we had tried and failed to be anything other than what we were: one gay, one, in the end, straight, and yet neither able to shake off the memory of the other, or of that summer in which we had felt, however foolishly, that we were rarefied, special. We had agreed, finally, to avoid definitions, which hurt us more than they helped; we spoke once a year, on New Year's Day, an uncanny day that is suspended, as we were, between then and now, there and here. "I'm getting married," he called to say to me, I who knew what his body tasted like, the salt of his mouth, the earthen smell between his legs. "And"—he cleared his throat—"we want you to be in the wedding. We want you to read something." I didn't say anything. "You're the writer; you think of something," he said, not joking but really irritated, gruff with embarrassment. He hung up. As it turned out, his fiancée had her own ideas about what I should read. I hadn't met her, didn't want to know about her. She wrote me, on thick creamy stationery with a monogram at the top, asking if I would read from the Song of Songs. "It would mean so much to us," she wrote in her sorority-girl writing, all fat loops and curls. Her conventionality made me feel powerful, inflated me with superiority and so made me forgiving. I agreed to read.

That was the first time I read the Song of Songs, the Song of Solomon, a song, according to one eighteenth-century Jewish commentator from Lithuania, that celebrates the union of the body, with its needs and desires, and the soul—Cupid and Psyche, once again; a poem, according to most other scholars, about being different from everyone else, the song, some scholars think, that is meant to be an allegory of a relationship unlike any other, between God and his disaster-prone people, a people at once chosen and cursed, a relationship so intense that only the metaphors of physical desire could do it justice. I read that day, per the bride's instructions, first in Hebrew, then in English. *Ani ḥabatseleṭ ha'Sharon,* I said in this old wooden church, staring straight at him, thinking of the first day I saw him, red hair dark with damp from the June heat, of Chouky's giggle in the background at someone's obvious dirty joke, a joke told over the vegetable terrine that a boy, now ten years dead, had labored over, trying to impress our glamorous friend who had lived so richly and so long; I thought of the poolside at Chouky's annual Labor Day party, littered with discarded bathing suits and shorts, of a waterbed rocking, of the salty taste of my friend's mouth in the dark. I thought of these and began my piece. *Ani ḥabatseleṭ ha'Sharon,* I said, loudly. *I am the Rose of Sharon . . .*

.   .   .

There is one more text apart from the inscriptions on my great-aunt's tombstone that is relevant to her death. I found it only recently, almost by accident, while doing some research on my father's family at City Hall.

The history of my mother's family, vain, meticulous, garrulous, had always been well documented. We know little, by comparison, of my father's uncles and aunts and grandparents. There is no family plot in an old cemetery somewhere; my father's parents lie in a carefully manicured "memorial park" in Miami, a cemetery where there are no headstones but instead low brass plaques. No one stands out; no one gets a high stone, let alone a rose.

It was ostensibly to recover my father's forgotten family —a family without myths and without photographs, about whom we knew very little—and, perhaps, to recover my father, that I'd come to the Municipal Archives down near City Hall, on a summer day in 1996. I spent half a day looking for the familiar last name, my name, duly noting dates of birth and death. But these people were, in the end, merely names to me. None had a picture; all those pictures had burned in a fire long before my father was even born. Too few of these lost Mendelsohns had stories; none had died of anything so wonderful as a broken heart, or a broken will. As I sat there looking at the microfilmed death certificate of my father's father's brother (died aged one and a half, of meningitis, in 1895), I thought about my great-aunt Ray, about beautiful death. So I put aside my father's family and began once again to think about my mother's, about my great-aunt's death. I wanted to see and read her death certificate. There was no reason to do this other than to be again in the presence of something to do with her death, although to shield myself from this knowledge, the knowledge that I was obsessed, I invented a pretext, something that would give my obsession the appearance of reason. I told myself that in all these years of hearing about her dying young, I'd never ascertained what it was she died of. Wasn't this strange? Wasn't this careless? Now I would learn.

At the Municipal Archives on Centre Street in downtown Manhattan, near City Hall, certificates of death are organized by number. In order to find one, you have to start with a name. If, say, you are looking for the death certificate of a Ray Jager, who died *ha'betulah*, unmarried, on the third of September in 1923, you'd first have to find the microfilm roll called "Manhattan Death Index 1923." This index lists, in alphabetical order, the names of all people who died in Manhattan in 1923 for whom death certificates were registered. The name of each dead person is cross-referenced with the number of that person's death certificate, which you then have to locate on another microfilm, which will have a title like "Manhattan Deaths #22345–25346." (The same procedure will get you births and marriages too.) This is all easy enough, and it's how I managed to find the death certificates for my father's lost aunts and uncles, the ones who died young, with no heroic narratives to immortalize them.

But it was less easy than I'd expected in the case of my great-aunt Ray, because the Manhattan Death Index 1923 doesn't list any deceased person by the name of Ray Jager. Nor Ray Jaeger. Nor Ray Yaeger nor Yager nor Rae or even Rachel with any of those last names either.

There seemed to be no record of her death.

At first I was unperturbed, accustomed as I was to the strange things that can happen to very old texts. So I set to work, using, to find this dead Jewish girl, the techniques of philology and paleology I'd learned to study the Greeks. First I checked once again all the variant spellings of her first and last names; this again turned up nothing. Then I checked the Death Indices for 1921, and 1922, and 1924, and even 1932, thinking that the certificate had somehow been misfiled by date, but there was still no record that anyone by that name, or any of its possible variants, had died on the third of September, or indeed in any month, in any of those years. Finally, I (who, like my father, hate asking for help) asked the clerk at the desk, who said he could not help me. If the certificate had been misfiled, he said cheerfully, there was no way to find it. I wondered briefly what my grandfather would have done, faced with this chipper clerical recalcitrance; I didn't doubt he would have found a way to make the clerk find it.

As a last resort, I decided to check under what would have been Ray's married name, which was her mother's maiden name, M———. I reasoned that, since she had after all died so shortly before she was to have been married, perhaps there had been a misfiling of name, rather than date.

In this, it turned out, I was right. The Manhattan Death Index 1923 does list a death certificate, #22———, for a Ray M———, who died 3 September 1923.

Here is the strange part, the part that made me realize that her monument was a lie: the strange thing was not the incorrect last name of the deceased, which after all could have been the result of a confused clerk faced with the tortured over-explanation of a distraught family member—perhaps even my grandfather?—but what was written beside the line for "Occupation at the Time of Death." The strange thing was that on this line they had written "Housewife."

There is, in the Municipal Archives in downtown Manhattan, another registry besides the Death Index. This one is called the Bride's Registry. Like the Death Index, this registry provides a listing by last name and year that can be cross-referenced with a certificate number, although of course in this case the certificate is a happy one, of marriage, rather than a tragic one, of death. The Bride's Registry provides the full maiden name of every woman married in New York City between 1847 and 1937; beside her name, the number of the marriage certificate is listed, and using this number you can find the certificate and, if you like, view it on a large, unwieldy, gunmetal-gray projector. For the year 1922, under the letter J, the Manhattan Bride's Registry lists a Ray Jager, whose marriage was recorded on certificate number 10———.

This certificate is dated the eighteenth of February 1922. It attests the marriage, on that day, between Ray Jager and her first cousin Sam M———. The signatures of the bride and groom on this certificate are legible, as are the signatures of the two witnesses. One of these witnesses was the groom's sister— as it happens, the same pinched, matronly woman who was unlucky enough to share that early 1915 photograph with a radiant, nineteen-year-old Ray. The other witness to this marriage, a marriage that my grandfather had told me on countless occasions had never taken place, a marriage supposedly postponed and then canceled, a marriage that set in motion hatreds that would last three generations—the other witness to this marriage was one well known to me. I had seen the powerful, loping writing at the bottom of dozens of letters over the years, letters written with a bulbous black Parker fountain pen in an old-fashioned medium-blue ink. I didn't have to read the name at the bottom of the certificate. The other witness was my grandfather.

The case for the perfection of Sophocles' *Antigone,* that play whose protagonist is a bride of death, has traditionally stumbled on what is called "the question of the double burial." The problem may be summarized as follows:

After the opening scene, in which Antigone quarrels with her more practical sister Ismene, Antigone goes off, presumably to perform the forbidden burial. And indeed, soon afterwards we hear, from one of the guards who have been posted near the site where the body of Polynices is meant to remain unburied, that a marvelous thing had happened: someone has crept up, somehow unnoticed, and performed a token burial of the stinking body: the scattering of some dust, a small ablution. An enraged Creon orders that the body be stripped of its meager dirt and once again guarded, and threatens the guards with terrible tortures if they fail again to make sure that the traitor's body remains unburied. It is during this second watch that the guards (and, by extension, we, the audience) catch Antigone stealing towards the body and performing the ritual.

The problem for critics of the play is that if it was Antigone who performed the first burial—the one the messenger had already described—why return for a second? The religious obligation that impels her to endanger her life would have required the merest symbolic burial, which has, as we know, already been performed. So the question is, Why the second burial? Why return to see the dead body once more? Why come back?

After learning that the photograph on Ray's tombstone was, in fact, an image of a married woman, not a virgin after all, not a bride of death, I tried to find out what I could about the characters in a drama that had suddenly taken a bizarre turn, a drama that might be turning out to be about something entirely other than what I'd always thought it was about. A few summers ago I finally met the daughter of the woman who married Ray's fiancé—no, her *husband*. She lives now in Tennessee, has made the transition that I would later make, from North to South, from the place where Jews live to the place where Gentiles live, and it is possible, looking at her smooth and fine-featured face, to see her dead mother, my other beautiful great-aunt. The daughter (like the mother, I have heard) has skin so clear it is almost translucent. This woman, born three years after Ray died, is in her late sixties now, three times as old as her mother was when she was forced to marry the man who had, as it turns out, already married her sister. Like my parents, this woman grew up in New York City—my father lived across the street from her long before he knew my mother, and remembers the day when the ambulance pulled up to take away a woman with fine features and translucently fair skin, dead at thirty-five of a stroke—but her long years in a distant Southern state have left their mark, and she speaks with an accent not at all unlike those of the mothers of the beautiful blond Tennesseeans and Georgians and Alabamians I knew at school. It was odd, that day, to hear her speaking of Hebrews, of people called *Ruchel* and *Necha* and *Shmuel*, in that voice, the voice I had come to associate with Gentiles and with pleasure.

She wanted to talk about her father, as it turned out, which disappointed me because ugliness did not interest me, and her father—the object of my grandfather's loathing—was famously ugly. I wanted to hear about the beauty of her aunt and her mother. But she talked about her father, of whom I'd heard so often from my grandfather, and been satisfied to hear, that he was ugly, and small, and had smallpox scars, and had in some indistinct way been responsible for the deaths of my two great-aunts. My grandfather sneered whenever he spoke of this man, who was the only person in our family to decline to be buried in that plot in Brooklyn—had insisted, in fact, on cremation, which is forbidden by the Jewish law that consigned all the others to the familiar plot of ground. When I heard this last detail as a child, listening to my grandfather and absorbing his inflections, I assumed that my great-uncle (who was also my first cousin twice removed) had wanted to be cremated in order to eradicate the ugliness with which he'd been cursed and which had made him so obviously an outsider in my grandfather's beautiful family. It turned out I was wrong.

In fact, it turned out I was, once again, wrong about a great deal. His daughter (who, because her parents were first cousins, is both my first cousin once removed and my second cousin once removed) told me other things. That her father was a great reader, for instance, and that in this he had much in common with the long-dead Ray; during their engagement, they had enjoyed talking about books. *During their engagement they had talked about books? They had talked?* My grandfather had never mentioned this, had never suggested that they had had anything like a relationship. "Oh, yes," this soft Southern voice said to me, "it was a real love match." She went on to say that her father had been a freethinker, had rejected the stultifying strictures of his family's Orthodox faith, which my grandfather followed even in death . . .

. . . For instance: one summer's day when I was fourteen I returned to my parents' house, where my grandfather was staying that summer, from the house where a schoolmate of mine lived, a boy a couple of years older to whom I barely spoke in school but with whom—this went on for about a year—I would get together every few days and we would undress and masturbate, in complete, ecclesiastical silence, in his basement after watching TV for a few minutes. My grandfather summoned me into my room and pointed to the old Underwood that had been his secretary's at the passementerie factory and had me type up a document listing in elaborate detail the instructions for the tending of his body after his death. My own body still humming with the orgasm I had had minutes before, I sat and typed, enjoying my secret. As I learned that day, my grandfather would be as vain in death as he was in life. When he died, he said to me—motioning for me to write as he lay on his back on my hard, cotlike bed, his pinkie ring winking in the afternoon light—when he died his body was to be washed by the people of the congregation whose job it was to see to this ritual, and then, through the night between his death and his burial, it was to be watched by the old men of his congregation, men who recited certain prayers as they kept their vigil; if he were to die in Florida, as he expected to, the body was to be flown back as soon as legally permitted so that burial could take place, as ritual dictated, within twenty-four hours of death; that in conformance with the law, no autopsy was to be performed; that the body was to be wrapped in a tallis and placed in a plain wooden box and lowered into the ground that held his wife and his mother and his beautiful sisters and his brother and the cousins whom he'd hated, had ceased speaking to after that wartime Thanksgiving dinner at which the youngest sister, forced to marry the same cousin who'd married the eldest, had died, suddenly, of a stroke, at thirty-five, a death that my grandfather blamed on the hated, ugly cousin; and, finally, that at the moment of his death a certain sum of money was to be sent to a religious order in Jerusalem whose adherents, in return for this gift, would then say prayers for the repose of his soul every day for a year after his death.

Six years later almost to the day, as it happened, after I typed that document, my grandfather died in the swimming pool, exhausted and emaciated by the cancer that was eating his stomach. *His stomach was being eaten:* for him, who had been so finicky about what he put in his stomach, the Glatt kosher delicacies and the tiny peas, this was not without a certain macabre humor. The last time I heard his voice, in June of 1980, I'd picked up the telephone in my parents' house to make a call and instead heard voices on the line: my grandfather talking heatedly with my mother. By this point, of course, we all knew he was dying; it was just a matter of time. *I can't eat,* he was saying, loudly, *I can't drink, and I can't shit. What the hell's the point?*

So my grandfather died in his own way, demanding and willful to the end, insisting on the time and place, just as he had insisted on everything else. The arrangements he'd dictated to me took place more or less in conformity with his wishes. The body was tended, bathed, washed, wrapped, transported, delivered. The coffin, I noticed at the burial, was not entirely plain: a Star of David was carved into the curved top. But it was wooden, otherwise unadorned, would revert to the earth quickly, which was the point of wood rather than metal. I glimpsed the star just briefly, as the shovelful of red earth I'd been instructed to throw in hit the coffin with a dull gravelly thud and hid the star. The noise was shocking, and for the first time I realized he was truly dead. How were we to think of him, on this hot June day, of him who had always dictated and exacted and demanded and insisted and amused and entertained and lied, as merely a thing in a box? A box that we were now covering with earth as my mother, holding a snapshot of him in which he's dressed in a mustard-and-white argyle sweater and matching mustard pants, alternately wept (furiously, an only child now orphaned) and laughed at the memory of his famous jokes, as did some of the others who knew him. A box that we were now covering with earth until, before our eyes, the hole was filled up and he was gone, had become a site rather than a person. Now he was like the others, he had become his inscription and his photograph and his stories.

A few weeks after this I heard odd noises coming from my mother's room. This was the room in which I'd spent so much secret time as a child, the room with the long mirror. Choked with embarrassment—no child likes to be reminded of his parent's physicality—I thought I'd walk by, ignoring the sound, but again I heard it, this strangled noise, and so went in, and there on her bed was my mother, weeping, and I asked her what was the matter, and she looked up and told me what she hadn't told us before, which was that because my grandfather had been a suicide, had drowned himself and his cancerous tumor in the cool water of the swimming pool that Friday the thirteenth in June, they had had to perform an autopsy. "It's the law," my mother said, and started crying again. I tried to soothe her, to tell her it didn't matter now, that she had to obey the law, that it couldn't make a difference now he was in the ground, and she looked up at me again, weeping and laughing at the same time, and said, "Daddy's going to *kill* me."

So this was my grandfather, the good guy, the hero of the stories in which the malformed, scarred cousin who had married two of his sisters, the beautiful ones, had been the villain.

Because that man was the first cousin of his bride, everyone in our family is two things at once: the bride's father-in-law was also her uncle; my grandfather's first cousin was also his brother-in-law; my mother's first cousin, the product of that union, was simultaneously her second cousin. We are always two things at once. Now my mother's cousin, the daughter of the second ill-fated wedding between my grandfather's beloved sister and his loathed cousin, went on talking . . .

She said that her father, the bad guy, had abandoned his religion, had sought other explanations, other outlets; he had been a member of the Ethical Culture Society, followed politics intently, was a person of the left. He was bad with money, she said; he gambled, gave donations of money to the poor, contributed unwisely to unpopular political causes. She said that he was not like the other people in this family. He had friends who were black. He had friends, she said, looking at me with gentle meaningfulness, who were homosexuals. He was not like the others, not at all like my grandfather, my Orthodox grandfather, who did not really read that much, who told *faygeleh* jokes, jokes about boys who liked other boys, boys like me; not at all like my grandfather, who had never told me these things about the man about whom, in his telling of his tales, he said very little except that he was ugly, was small, and had smallpox scars.

How do you learn about lies? Sometimes you find out accidentally; sometimes you have to be told. Sometimes you learn for yourself that the stories you needed to believe were, in the end, myths, or merely lies.

Because I am gay, I know about the lies that must be told, and I have felt, too, the fascination exerted by certain myths; I know why people invent them. I know, for instance, about the seductive myth of exceptionality, the legend that my school friends and I had unwittingly been acting out during that summer of Ionic columns and rare wines, a story we tell about how special and knowledgeable we are, a story in which we wear the most fashionable clothes, eat at the fanciest restaurants (which we know about and others may not), have access to the most sought-after concerts and parties, know—instinctively, some would say—about the best and most beautiful objects, apartments, beaches, resorts: Heywood-Wakefield rather than IKEA, rent-controlled prewar buildings instead of white-brick boxes, St. Bart's instead of, say, Jamaica, the places and things other people haven't found out about yet, haven't been able to intuit. In reaction to our terrible adolescences, perhaps, which permanently shamed us, we have elevated the uncommon, the rare, the élite.

And yet the flip side of this is the culture of secrets, secret places, places in the dark. Betraying their origins in shame and concealment, most gay bars are still narrow and small, spaces hidden away from the street, the windows in the door painted over, the entryways covered from within by a curtain or a shutter. Walking from these hidden entrances to the bar itself always seems like running a gauntlet of sorts. Men line the walls, stand there with drinks or beer bottles at hip height, and with ostentatious nonchalance they track your passage with appraising eyes even as they school their faces to a careful self-protective disdain, the aloof look being one you have seen, of course, on a tombstone, and the ostensible disdain a strategy you learned early on when you realized you couldn't have the boys you really loved or when the father you wanted to impress ridiculed you. Given the overabundance of the accoutrements of pleasure—drinks, music, campy videos playing on the monitors screwed into the walls (in one video clip I saw fairly frequently, right before I stopped going out and switched to meeting men on-line, which has the virtues both of self-protection and of efficiency, one scene—a moment in the Joan Crawford biopic *Mommie Dearest* in which Faye Dunaway viciously smacks the girl who plays her daughter across the face while saying, "Why can't you just give me the *respect* that I deserve?"—plays over and over again, the repeats getting shorter and shorter until all you'd hear for about thirty manic seconds was the syllable *-pect* accompanying the sound and image of flesh hitting flesh until the violence had lost all context and became weirdly funny)—given the drinks and the music and the video monitors and the humor, there are surprisingly few real smiles. I have always been struck by this, by the grim unattainability that is the self-presentation of choice in gay bars, where the subject at hand is the very serious one of sexual pleasure. I find that I can relax here. I can relax because I understand (because I have long lived there, because this is the point of the lie) the world in which the important thing is to be seen, to be the object, not the subject, of desire, to be aloof, to be wanted for *being* aloof, for being a beautiful image suspended before the eyes of others, unsmiling, far more likely to haunt the memories of those who see me if I remain unknown and untouched than I would if they were to have me.

I have, of course, like most of the gay men I know, spent a good deal of time complaining about the bar scene. The complaining—that if you're a single gay man the only way to meet other single gay men, the only way to find someone to play with, is to stray into that familiar space, probably ugly, most likely badly lighted, filled with strangers and the music you wouldn't choose yourself, and wait against a wall with the drink in your hand until you finally slide into a conversation with someone whom you can't see quite well enough and who is probably only looking for a one-night stand anyway, unlike you who, you tell yourself, are looking for a Relationship—this complaint is a necessary lie. A lie, because I am pretty sure by now that we go to these places in order *not* to connect, but rather to exist in the exquisite moment when our desirability is still perfect, unspoiled by contact; necessary, because who could acknowledge that this was what he really wanted—to be a flawless image rather than a living person, to have a narrative rather than a life, to be tragic rather than to live—and not go mad?

For a long time after I learned the truth about my grandfather, I still tried to construct a narrative about his lie that would somehow preserve him in his glamour and authority.

To be fair, it was not only my grandfather who'd lied. His youngest sister lied too—the sister who became the substitute bride, the one who married the man who had earlier married her sister. And he, the ugly bridegroom, had lied too. Together they lied to their child, the one I had spoken with, my mother's cousin, who didn't know that her father had been married to her aunt for nearly two years, before the aunt had died so famously young and beautiful, so tragically, a week before her wedding. On her parents' wedding certificate, a document I have also looked at, hungry for some information that might yet allow me to preserve the tragic story, there is a space after the words "Number of Previous Marriages," and her father, briefly forgetting himself, had written "0," only to scratch a line through the hollow digit and replace it with a delicate, slightly shaky "1." This error gave me hope: if you yourself can forget you were married, maybe the real lie wasn't that you'd never married the girl, but that you *had* married her . . . unless, of course, this man who had married two sisters was so used to lying that he had begun to lie here, too, but was, perhaps, too intimidated by the context, the official and legal setting, the certificate, the judge.

The distant brother in Israel and his fierce beak-nosed wife lied as well, to their two children, who believed the same story that their American cousins had been told, and who, incidentally, do not bear the family name, are not called Jaeger, because after the Second World War nobody wanted to have German names. We cannot know whether the eldest brother, Sam, lied to his four nameless daughters, but there is no reason to suppose that they didn't lie as well. And the middle sister also lied, this time to her son, my mother's cousin, who was as incredulous as my mother had been on that afternoon when I called her from the pay phone outside of the Municipal Archives to tell her about her father's lie. "That's impossible," she said, flatly. "Have you told your Uncle Allan?" she went on, referring to her cousin, the son of the middle daughter, the one who thought she was ugly, the one who lived. "He'd know." What struck me, as I listened to the incredulous reactions of the children of the dead girl's sisters and brothers, was the realization that Ray's siblings, all of them dead by this point and therefore maddeningly distant, secretive now beneath their own stone monuments, side by side with the husbands they thought were beneath them or the wives they had kept secrets from, had long ago coordinated their lies, agreed on a story that made sense to them—*the beautiful girl, oppressed, heroic, died a week before her wedding,* the story that to me had meant *tragedy and loss are beautiful*—and had carefully fed that story to their children, who only now, far older than their parents were when they started the lies, and only because this lost girl and her tragic death were somehow so close to the core of who I was that I had wanted to experience her death for myself, these deceived children, now approaching old age themselves, were finally learning the truth.

Why had they all lied to their children, to their grandchildren, taken the trouble and expense to erect a monument that bore a false name, the maiden name of the girl who was no maiden when she died, a year after and not a week before her wedding?

Perhaps, I thought, it was the family's desire to expunge the memory of the unwanted marriage. Or perhaps there had been something about her death that they wanted erased from the record, something that otherwise would have haunted them and their youngest daughter, who was to marry the same man, in years to come—an adultery, a stillborn child, something perhaps worse . . . ? This line of explanation, I later realized, was one my grandfather might have come up with —filled with high emotion and low motives, a good melo-dramatic tale to spin over dinner with your nephews and grandchildren wide-eyed and silent with the pleasure of the narrative.

I thought of something else, too, and it was this thought that lingered in my mind for months, until I hit upon what must have been the truth—a truth that seemed clear only after I had learned more about the man who was my grandfather. It occurred to me, and I told other people this, shared it with them because, if anything, it only further enhanced the mystery of these dead people—it occurred to me that instead of serving to erase some terrible secret, something that had happened, perhaps the lie that my grandfather had told me was meant to serve something less concrete: an idea of themselves that the family needed to maintain in order to go on, a myth they wanted to remain untouched by what had actually happened. Maybe they'd put up the tombstone with its lies about virginity and grief because they'd decided that the wedding to the ugly cousin should never have taken place to begin with. Maybe they had erected a virgin's monument over a married woman because they wanted to maintain in her death what they could not maintain during her life, which was the myth of their distinctness from ugliness, their aloofness from a squalor so terrible that it could force you to sell your own child, sacrifice your beautiful eldest daughter, your rose, to your need to survive.

Of course, this explanation, in its way, also preserves the mythic aspect of the story, and hence of my grandfather's family, because even as it pretends to take away from their aloofness, their superiority, their aristocratic pretensions ("*Everyone* had servants in the old country," my father, whose family had no pretensions, would say, rolling his eyes, when he wanted to tease my mother in the middle of some story about her family), it gives them something equally resonant and beautiful: it makes them into the authors of their own histories, the scribes of their own myth.

As it turned out, it was none of these things.

A few months after I discovered what I thought to be my grandfather's lie, I started thinking—not in words, the rich and seductive words my grandfather might use ("secret," "reputation," "revenge"), but in numbers. I began, in other words, to think like the mathematician, like my father, and like the mother of the child to whom I had connected my life. Ray had come to the States in 1915; her secret husband was a naturalized citizen. Her sister, the "ugly" one, and her brother, who became my grandfather, had arrived together in 1920;

the rest of the siblings, and the mother, in 1922. Perhaps, it occurred to me, she'd needed to establish citizenship herself in order for these relatives to get visas? Perhaps the first, February 1922, wedding was a bureaucratic maneuver meant to ensure that the mother—a saint by all accounts, but of course how not, since she died fairly young, too—the mother and the children would be able to stay, stay with a daughter who was a citizen.

The answer finally came, as it happened, from AOL. In response to a query I'd posted on the Internet, I received an E-mail from a woman who was knowledgeable about the history of immigration law. It was from this woman that I first learned about the Emergency Quota Act, which, when it took effect in May 1921, created a panic in the immigrant community. Rumors—most of them untrue, as it happened—flew back and forth among recent immigrants to the United States, especially those who, like my great-aunt, had relatives in Eastern Europe still waiting to come over. There were rumors that, henceforth, only men would be able to immigrate; that wives and children would not be permitted to come unless their husbands or fathers were already in America; that people emigrating from Eastern Europe wouldn't be able to know for sure whether they'd be allowed into the United States until they actually arrived. But most important, for me, was the rumor my correspondent saved for last. Like a lot of people at the time (she wrote), my great-aunt may have heard the rumor that if she was married to a U.S. citizen, her parents and siblings could be admitted to the United States.

Another woman, an authority on Jewish religious law, told me something else, setting another piece of the puzzle into place: that Orthodox Jews like my grandfather and his sister and his cousins would not have considered a courthouse wedding to be valid; whatever her fiancé might later think, only the religious wedding, performed by a rabbi, was valid.

So that was it. That explained why the wedding invitations I have in my possession are for a spring 1923 date, even though the couple had been married by a judge the year before. The weddings for which the invitations had been printed was the real wedding, the Jewish wedding, the religious ceremony. This in turn would explain the maiden name on the monument, since they wouldn't have considered her truly married without the religious ceremony, the ceremony that had indeed had to be delayed from May to September of 1923 because of the bride's illness, the ceremony that indeed finally was canceled because she had died.

So maybe they had all been telling the truth as far as they were concerned—my grandfather, his sisters and brothers, the cousins, the children of the cousins. Maybe, for them, it hadn't been a lie.

But even as I write this, and see that it makes a flat and natural kind of sense, accounts for all the known facts in a coherent and intellectually satisfying way, I realize I'm disappointed. To lose the beautiful myth of who your family is, who you are—beautiful, oppressed, iconic, the aloof object of other people's envious fascination—lose it not to some story that was even deeper and perhaps even more satisfying, because it was a richer, better story—a story of cover-ups, stillborn babies, abuse, secrecy, shame—but to the dull realities of lived life, to immigration and visas and the practical need to work the system, to get by—; to lose your beautiful myth is terrible. Without it, how do you know who you are?

I have always thought, and wanted to think, that this girl's story was a tragedy, a myth of beauty and of loss; have always been intrigued, not just by the mysterious beauty of the girl who, as in all tragedies, I knew must die, but by the beauty *of her mystery,* by the enticing narrative about a secret and a lie. How typical that even now I want to cling to some other explanation, something more dramatic, more beautiful in the telling, something that will entertain, that will preserve my family's aloofness, its distinction, something that will, in its way, save *me.* Even if I know it isn't true. Maybe this is what my grandfather understood: Isn't a good story worth a lie?

Solutions to the "problem of the double burial" in Sophocles' *Antigone* have been ingenious. Perhaps, some have argued, there was some ritual act that had been left undone the first time? Perhaps some other ritual requirement, of which we are now ignorant, necessitated the second sprinkling of dust and water? Perhaps, most ingeniously, the first burial wasn't actually performed by the defiant girl, but by the gods themselves?

Yet for all my interest in burials and beautiful heroic dead girls, I never really saw the double burial as a problem. This was partly because I tend to be more interested in the drama than in logic—more like my mother than my father, maybe. And partly because, in another way, the second burial always made a kind of sense to me. After all, fulfillment of the rite and duty to family were only one of Antigone's missions in the play. Her other mission, the mission that seemed so natural to me that I never even thought this famous problem *was* a problem, the mission without which there would be no play, was to get caught, to be noticed, so that she might die. For in dying she could become a bride of death, an everlasting part of the myth. Beautiful, and dead.

V. IDENTITIES

I thought once that I wanted to die. On a summer afternoon that turned out to be the last time I was with the red-haired boy, I walked a hundred blocks uptown and then another hundred downtown, through the night and morning, thinking of ways to kill myself. I thought I had to kill myself because I thought I had to be one thing, a man who could wholly possess the thing he wanted in a way that was continuous with who he was. And this, it was clear, was impossible.

But instead of suicide, of myth and a monument, what evolved was this: a compromise. After that last time, we agreed to our special arrangement, our yearly conversation on New Year's Day, as if our time together had initiated some intimacy that could never be expressed physically but that needed a controlled outlet. And so every year on the first day of the year the phone in whichever of my two spaces I happen to be in will ring, and it will be him, now back in Richmond, gradually becoming his own father, dating girls, telling me about them—desultory talk about nothing in particular until the end of the conversation when he will say, suddenly, "Well, talk to you next year."

You find a way to compromise. You stare longingly at the figure in the distance, the beautiful image that you found, one day, in a classroom or a cemetery, when you didn't even know what it was you were looking for, but you move on. You find the spaces in between, and you live.

You may have to live in two places. One of these places may be in New York City, slightly to the north of gay culture. Your closets may be filled with beautiful clothes, clothes that remind you of your vain and thrilling grandfather, who turned out, perhaps, to be no more of a liar than anyone is, really; you may think of him each morning as you put on your socks and undershorts and cologne in the way he told you to, the way that left the crease in your pants crisp, the way that prepared you best to charm and seduce. In it, you might enjoy pagan pleasures, the pleasures of vanity and of multiplicity, of seeking through a crowded place—the thick wood of myth transformed into the denseness that is the city—of seeking the face that haunts your imagination, hovering in the distance at the edge of things, the face of beauty and impossibility, one you know you can't quite have even as you keep reaching for it, falling through the bodies that go with the faces, back into yourself, again and again. You might find the pleasure in this, and find yourself happy in a way that is different from the happiness you learned about when you were growing up in a very different place.

The other place you live might be an hour's train ride from your apartment in the city, a place not that different from the quiet suburb where you grew up and where, on a street where every house was exactly the same, you absorbed the myths of exceptionality, the myths by which your strange and difficult family had always lived, the myths your beautiful mother told herself as she folded towels amidst the blue glass objects that surround her, myths spun by her father with his many wives and his starched shirts, his stories and his brilliantine and his lies. This place may be a place like the one in which you feared your father, who invented no myths but instead struggled to build things, to fix automobiles and make music and fires, to create something not for or of himself but for his children, who were also his creations. In this place you may teach classics, which allows you to remember your Greeks, with their precise grammars and their statues that even when broken are beautiful and whole, even as you live the life of your Hebrews, a life of children and holidays and messes, a life in which you know that one day the child whose birth you witnessed will be there when you are not, will bury you, will watch as you disappear into the same Jewish earth that already holds the man who told you beautiful stories and the girl he told stories about.

You may make other compromises. On the first day of every year, you may speak to the bridegroom whom you once thought you loved, speak to him on this day and no other, a stricture like something out of a fairy tale—*a hundred years of sleep and one of wakefulness*—which allows you to keep your impossible love at the periphery of your life but not in it, a figure at the edge looking towards the center. During the rest of the year you may fall in love with other men, or merely sleep with them, but at any rate you will realize that you enjoy them. In one of these places you may love your boys, your men who are boys, yearn for and sometimes possess their bodies, while in the other you may spend your time caring for a small child, a little boy, while living there with his mother, with a woman.

You move between two places. You move between two

places. You are, after all, the one whose name enfolds the mysteries of *men* and *de,* of repetition that is also opposition, of one thing that can also be two. This is who you are; this is the grammar of your identity. It is not easy, it is not comfortable, it is not what you thought things were going to be like. But this is how it is, and when all is said and done—*in fin dei conti,* as the pale Italian boy I once loved would say, as, after sex, his voice lapping the air the way the water licks the stone in the city where he was born, he finished one of the elaborate stories he would tell about his family's history, stories that for all I know may have been lies contrived to keep me there at his side once desire was spent—*at the end of all these tales* you live in the middle voice, you are here and you are there, living in both these places, moving between them, you are here and you are there, you are sometimes the rose and sometimes the rock, sometimes the photograph and sometimes the person, the monument but also the girl, object and subject, a boy and a man, you are sometimes cruel and sometimes wounded, sometimes the beauty and sometimes the loss, you are here and you are there, and you are alive.

ACKNOWLEDGMENTS

My parents, Marlene and Jay Mendelsohn, have been the source of everything: inspiration, support, above all the sense, instilled early on, of what an interesting and useful life could be like. To my brothers, sister, and sisters-in-law I turned gratefully and often over the past few years: Andrew Mendelsohn and Virginia Shea; Matthew Mendelsohn and Maya Vastardis; Eric Mendelsohn; and Jennifer Mendelsohn. To my brother Eric, especially, I owe more than I can say here; in certain ways, this book is as much his as mine.

All of my friends, as usual, ended up being pressed into midwife duty, but a small circle in particular gave me more support, and were more generous and patient, than I sometimes deserved: Hilton Als, Marc Angers, W. C. Blackstone, Jenny Strauss Clay, Spencer Cox, Diane Feldman, Charles Flowers (Rhoda, *not* Mary), Bob Gottlieb, Renée Guest, Brooks Peters, Sarah Pettit, Kate Sekules, Gordon VeneKlasen, Froma Zeitlin, and, above all, Lily and Peter Knezevich, *sine quibus non*. Technically, I'm not supposed to include Patti Hart in the "friends" category, but the writing of this book, and much that is in it, would not have been possible without her, either. And I'd be remiss if I didn't mention the crucial distractions afforded by the First Friday gang and, especially, the Sunday Schlockers; they know who they are.

I am also deeply grateful to Glen Bowersock and to Louis Begley, whose efforts on behalf of this book following its hardcover publication have meant much to me, and whom indeed I am now able to count among my friends.

The idea of writing a book like this is one I owe to the early encouragement of Robert Weil; and Camille Paglia, to whom, indeed, I owe several crucial opportunities, found me the perfect agent. The unflagging good spirits and efficiency of Sita White and Kerry Smith at Artists Agency have made business a virtual pleasure; and at Knopf, Sarah McGrath, Webb Younce, and especially the formidably gifted Ben Moser have made my working life considerably smoother than it otherwise would have been. The period following the original publication of this book also made me aware of how indebted I am to Gabrielle Brooks, Nicholas Latimer, and William Loverd; they're as delightful to know as they are to work with. I want especially to acknowledge my debt to Jordan Pavlin, without whose enthusiasm and patience this book would never have existed in the first place. Many thanks, too, to Edward Kastenmeier at Vintage for making the transition from cloth to paper a seamless and extremely pleasant one. Finally, and most importantly, Robin Desser is what every writer wishes for in an editor. It took us twenty years to end up together, but I think she'll agree that it was *bashert*.

It is to Lydia Wills that I owe the most. I hope she'll forgive me a cliché, but she believed in this book, and in me, even when I didn't; she knew better than (and before) I did what it really was, and worked hard for it to be allowed to take its proper shape. She's a wonderful agent, and a treasured friend.

Printed in the United States
by Baker & Taylor Publisher Services